PRELUDE

Bratislava is a great city to visit. It has a hundreds of interesting places to visit. The atmosphere is magical and the culture is mesmerizing. Bratislava was always an underdog overshadowed by Budapest, Vienna and Prague, but as you will soon discover it is just as beautiful and interesting.

Part of Bratislava's beauty is hidden in its history. Sure the view from the castle is great, but the visit is much more interesting when you notice that there is a gate beyond which there is only pure air and it becomes even more interesting when you read why in this book.

I had fun writing this book. My goal was to take all of the information about Bratislava, pick out the most interesting parts and compress it all into this small guide. I left the slushy phrases and insincerity to others.

I hope you will appreciate the effort that was put into this book and that at the end of your visit you will consider Bratislava to be as beautiful as I believe it to be.

Martin Gottweis

CONTENTS

What to Do 89

Leisure 101

Where to Stay 107

Eating and Drinking 111

Suggested Ittineraries 123

Street-finder 129

Index 131

HOW TO USE THIS BOOK

ICONS

The most important information is marked by clearly visible icons:

- months of operation
- opening hours
- phone number
- webpage
- € price
- more on page ..
- **MAP** location on map

ORIENTATION

For your convenience this book is divided into nine chapters; each full of interesting and useful information. The chapters are preceded by: a table of contents, highlights and a twelve-page map. You will find a street-finder and an index at the end of the book.

STREET-FINDER

The street-finder at the end of this book is a great tool when you know the street's name and wish to find it. The streets are listed alphabetically and the map reference utilizes a grid coordination system.

PRIVATE REFERENCES

To avoid discrimination, our policy is to never mention private companies; except for two exceptions.

The first exception is if the company offers a product that is unique and does not have much competition (e.g., boat trips or shopping malls).

The second exception is a paid review. Since reviewing all of the restaurants and hotels in Bratislava would be impossible, we charge a review fee for venues that wish to be reviewed and included in this book. This way all venues have a chance to be included and tourists receive better information since the venues which decide to be included in this book are well-established and know they will be around to receive the tourists.

ONLY ONCE

This book mentions every piece of information only once. For example, statue of French soldier could be included in both the article about the main square and in the section regarding statues.

MAP REFERENCES

To help you find your way around, 12 pages of maps have been included which are just before the main chapters.

There are two ways the objects are marked:

PIN

Some objects have their own pin in the map so you can find them fast and know exactly where those objects are.

For example, to find **MAP** ●1 you first need to go to the upper right-hand corner of the map that has a green tag and the object is under pin #1.

GRID

Not all objects can have a pin and those that do not have a pin can be found using a grid. The grid annotation gives a letter plus number combination.

For example, to find **MAP** ●F5 you first need to go to the map that has a green tag and the object is in column F, row 5.

 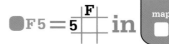

OPENING HOURS

Some venues' opening hours are rather complex, i.e., they are different for different days of the week and/or month. In this case, the opening hours stated are for the period when venue is always open.

For example, if a gallery is open from 10 a.m. - 8 p.m. on Tuesdays in July, but is only open from 8 a.m. - 4 p.m. on Saturdays in December, this book gives you ● 10:00 - 16:00; which means that when-

ever you come, the gallery should be open.

Oh, and since we are in Europe, the 24-hour format is used. If you haven't seen this before, just subtract 12 and you will get the p.m. time (e.g., 16:00 = 16-12 = 4 p.m.).

PRICES

As with opening hours, prices often differ based on time or season. Thus, if only one price is mentioned, it is the price you should expect.

BECOME AN EDITOR

Work with us on the future editions of this book. Have you had an experience in Bratislava that you liked, but a similar experience is not mentioned in this book? Have you found information in this book that is outdated? Or do you just have an idea about how to make this book better?

Write us at **goguide@souvenirxps.com** and if we use your tip we will thank you with a cool button badge.

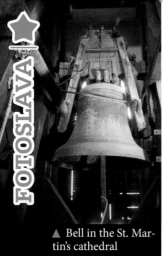

▲ Bell in the St. Martin's cathedral

▲ Vintage postcard - The synagogue was demolished in 1970

▼ December 4, 1989 - More than 200,000 people crossed the border for the first time

▼ Castle in 1966 before the New bridge was built **MAP** ▲L4

▼ Construction of the New bridge

▲ Notice the castle in a desolate condition

◀ Bratislava castle in 1964

▼ 1989 - Behind the border

Cars near the Michael's gate ▼

▲ Slovakia is one of the 10 countries the Danube flows through

◀ The luxurious interior of the Primate's palace

Museum of Natural History ▼

▼ Minor flooding of the left bank in 2006

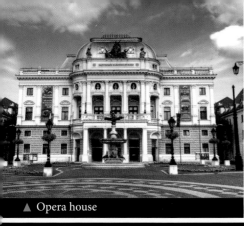

▲ Opera house

▲ Tower of the Franciscan church

▼ Bratislava as viewed from Petržalka

▼ The Old Town Hall and the Maximillian fountain on the Main Square

▲ Apollo Bridge - The newest bridge in Bratislava

◄ Peaceful nature, just minutes outside the city

▼ City-center

▼ The Old Bridge was built in 1890

▲ The New Bridge

▼ The Main Square

▲ Bratislava castle during sunset

▲ Communist housing solution

▼ Slovak Radio

▼ New Bridge at a foggy day

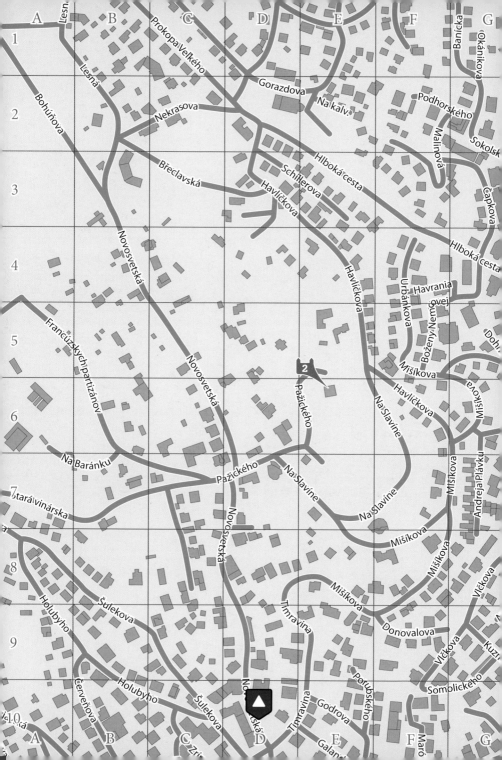

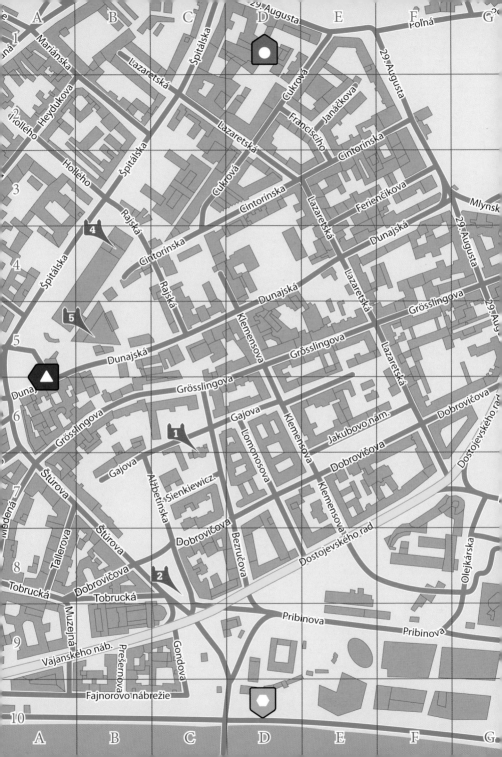

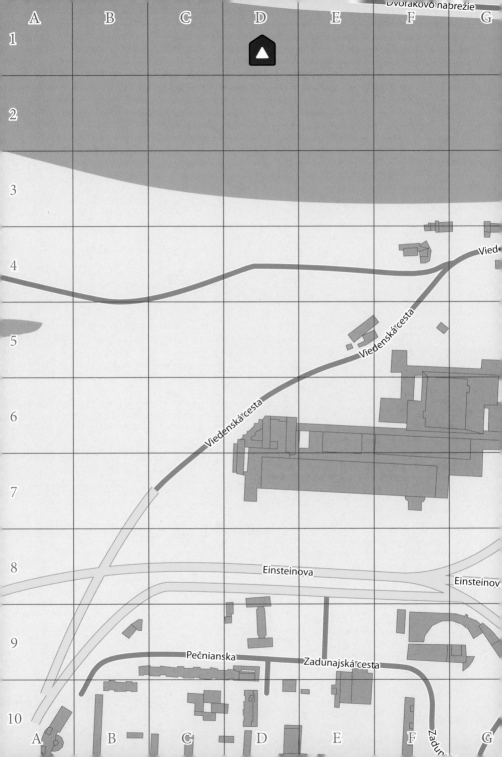

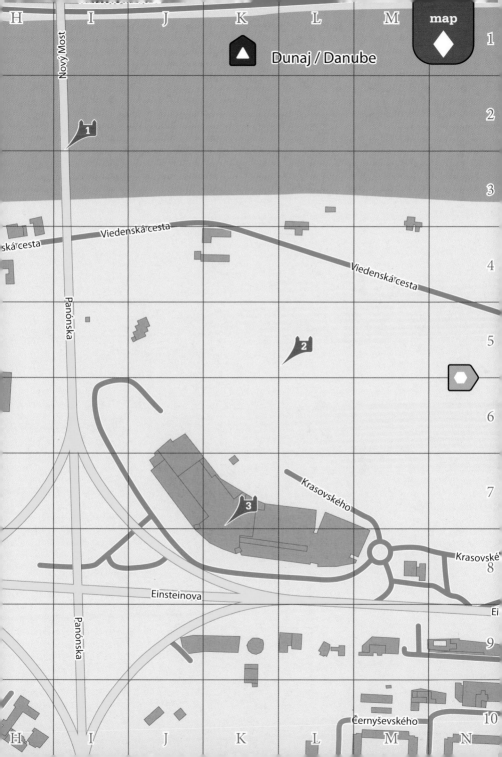

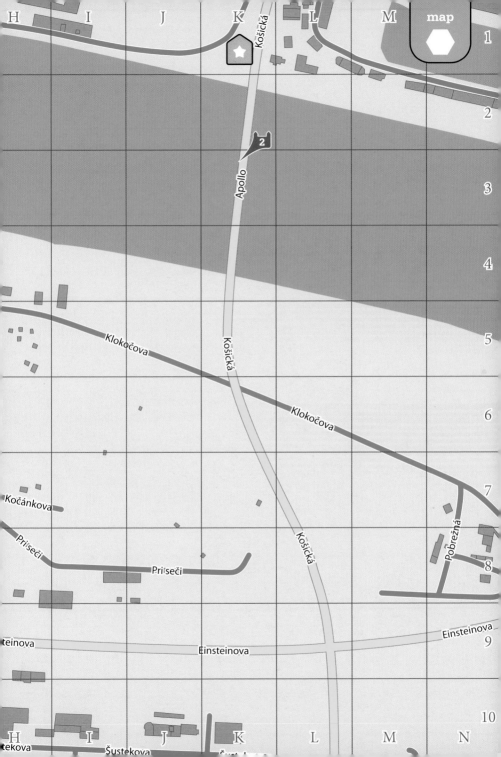

ABOUT BRATISLAVA

WHAT IS INTERESTING?

SEE THE HISTORY

In Bratislava, ten centuries can be seen in 30 minutes. Just take a walk through the city center. Notice the majestic castle, historic churches, beautiful Art Nouveau houses, hideous communist architecture and modern new buildings.

UNDERSTAND

Bratislava is the city of change. Bratislava was once the capital city of the Kingdom of Hungary. When this changed, all of the nobility moved out and the city started to deteriorate.

At the end of World War I, only 15% of the population were Slovaks; now it is 92%. Try to imagine how a city could change 80% of its population in such a short period of time.

The city also changed radically after the fall of communism. The majority of businesses are fairly new since private businesses did not exist at that time.

NO CARS

The city center retains its medieval look with quiet streets devoid of cars during the day. This provides a nice, calm atmosphere; which allows you to enjoy the architecture without the risk of being run over by incoming traffic.

Altogether, the city center provides 4.3 km

of pure European Renaissance sweetness. If this is not enough, enjoy a walk along the Danube or to the castle.

TINY CITY CENTER

The historical district in the city center is the smallest of all capital cities in Europe. The radius of the city center is only around 300 m. To compare, Vienna's district is approximately 900 m; making it 9 times larger in area. Although small, there is plenty to do and the city's atmosphere is incredible.

DANUBE

Having a river flowing right through the city center is great. On your visit, do not miss out and instead take a walk along the river or better yet, plan to have a riverside lunch.

COMMUNISM

If this is the first post-communist country you have visited, do not be surprised if Bratislava is not what you had expected. Most of the buildings in the city center were renovated and businesses are similar to what you would find elsewhere in Western Europe. If you are interested in what it once looked like, try to see buildings listed on page 📄 87. Some cities in Eastern Slovakia look exactly how they did before 1989.

▼ Bratislava Castle at Sunset as seen from Petržalka

THE DANUBE

FACT SHEET

Source:	Donaueschingen (Germany)
Mouth:	Danube Delta (Romania)
Length:	2,860 km (1,777 mi)
Discharge (Bratislava):	2025 m³/s
Depth (Bratislava):	3m (10 ft)
Maximum depth:	178 m
Countries:	🇩🇪 Germany, 🇦🇹 Austria, 🇸🇰 Slovakia, 🇭🇺 Hungary, 🇷🇸 Serbia, 🇭🇷 Croatia, 🇷🇴 Romania, 🇧🇬 Bulgaria, 🇲🇩 Moldova, 🇺🇦 Ukraine

The Danube was a long-standing border of the Roman Empire. Today it is the second longest river in Europe (after Volga) and is the longest river flowing through the European Union. The Danube flows through 4 capital cities, more than any other river in the world.

▲ The spring of the Danube in Donaueschingen

The Danube is used for freight transport and passenger cruises (📄 97). The river is navigated by barges heading toward Kelheim, Germany. The Rhine–Main–Danube Canal, built in 1992, connects the Danube with rivers Main and Rhine. This makes it possible to transport cargo from the Atlantic Ocean to inland Europe.

The Danube Bike Trail is a designated bicycle trail running along the river basin. The most popular section goes from Passau to Vienna and Bratislava (📄 103).

▲ Danube cruises are very popular

▼ Map of the Danube

HISTORY

PREHISTORY

The area of present-day Bratislava was inhabited as early as the Neolithic Age (9500 BC). These settlements were on the city's perimeter. In the Early Iron Age, the center of the settlements had shifted to where the present-day city center is. This occurred because of the strategic location of the hill and the river-crossing of the Danube. It is believe that a local Hallstatt culture prince resided here.

Around the year 100 BC, Celts formed an important Celtic oppidum, a fortified town, on the castle hill. This was the first time Bratislava had become a de facto town. Silver coins called Biatec were even minted here. Many of these coins were found on the castle hill and the motif

▲ Biatec - Celtic coins found in large numbers in Bratislava

from these coins now appears on the Slovak 5-koruna coin. It is believed that Biatec was the name of the Celtic prince who had organized the minting.

▼ Pavimentum - a mosaic-like flooring made by Romans found on the Castle hill

ROMAN EMPIRE

From the 1st century until the 4th, the border of the Roman Empire ran along the Danube. Several of these archaeological sites have been excavated; including Gerulata, a military camp near Rusovce (📄 91), and Devin Castle (📄 123); which was used by the Romans as a military garrison. The Roman settlement on the castle hill was called Pisonium.

SLAVS

The Slavs arrived during the 5th and 6th centuries. The first Slavic political entity, the Samo's Empire, was established in 623 when Samo had become the king of the Slavs. Later, Bratislava was part of Great Moravia. The first written reference of Bratislava is from the year 907 in connection with the Battle of Bratislava where the Magyars had defeated the Bavarians. This battle is considered as the end of Great Moravia, and Bratislava then became part of medieval Hungary.

BATTLEFIELD

Because of its strategic location, mostly because of the presence of the river-crossing, Bratislava became the site of frequent attacks and battles. It is believed that Bratislava Castle was one of the best fortified castles in the Kingdom of Hungary at that time. In 1030, Bratislava came under attack from the Czech Duke Břetislav I, but was able to hold off. Twelve years later, in 1042, Břetislav came back with the German armies of Henry III and this time he managed to take the city, but only temporarily. In 1052, Henry III returned and besieged the city for two months without success.

▼ Maria Theresa was coronated in Bratislava on June 25, 1741

This went on for centuries. For example, in 1526, after the battle of Mohacs where the Kingdom of Hungary was

▲ Painting of Bratislava in 1787

defeated, the Turks besieged Bratislava, but failed to enter the city.

CAPITAL CITY

After Budapest was captured by the Ottoman Empire, Bratislava was designated as the capital city of the Kingdom of Hungary in 1536. In addition, Bratislava became the meeting place of the Hungarian Diet and most importantly the city for coronation. Altogether, 11 kings and 8 consorts were coronated in St. Martin's Cathedral, Bratislava. Of those who were coronated, the most prominent was Maria Theresa whose coronation took place on June 25 1741.

RISE AND FALL

In 1782, Bratislava had around 33,000 inhabitants; making Bratislava the largest town in the Kingdom of Hungary. However, in 1783, Joseph II, son of Maria Theresa, had the crown jewels transported to Vienna and many of the governing offices moved back to Budapest. This caused most of the nobility to move either to Vienna or Budapest.

NAPOLEON

In 1805, Napoleon managed to defeat Austria in the Battle of Auster-litz. The peace treaty between France and Austria was signed in the Hall of Mirrors, in Primate's Palace (📖 63). A short four years later, Napoleon returned and walked through

▼ Cannonball in a wall - a memento from the French bombardment

▼ Devín Castle was destroyed in 1809 by the retreating forces of Napoleon I

the city after his armies had besieged, bombarded and finally conquered the city. Among others, the French armies managed to ruin Devín Castle (📄 123).

TURN OF THE CENTURY

After World War I, Austria-Hungary ceased to exist and the creation of Czechoslovakia was declared in Prague on October 28 1918. At that time, the population of Bratislava was

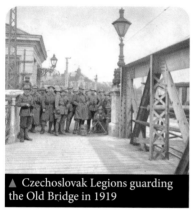

comprised of 42% Hungarians, 40% Germans and 15% Slovaks. The leaders of the city didn't want to be part of Czechoslovakia, so they declared Bratislava to be a free town named Wilson city, after American President Woodrow Wilson.

However, on January 1, 1919, it was taken by the Czechoslovak Legions. On February 12, the Hungarian and German people demonstrated on the present-day SNP Square against the Czechoslovak occupation. Czechoslovak troops shot and killed 9 demonstrators and wounded 23.

▲ Czechoslovak Legions guarding the Old Bridge in 1919

At this time, the official name of the city was changed to Bratislava instead of Prešporok (Slovak), Pressburg (German) and Pozsony (Hungarian).

Most of the remaining Germans and Hungarians were violently expelled by Slovak soldiers by the end of World War II.

COMMUNISM

After the Communists seized power in February 1948, the city became part of the Eastern Bloc. The first years were marked by the strong influence of the Soviet Union under the rule of Joseph Stalin. His paranoia resulted in staged trails for which many people were either sentenced to death or life imprisonment for absurd reasons.

In the early 1960s, the Czechoslovak economy became severely stagnant. The industrial growth rate was the lowest in Eastern Europe. Reform-minded Communists noticed this and used the situation to de-Stalinize Czechoslovakia. For example, the trials from years 1949-1954 were reviewed and some individuals were rehabilitated.

▲ Czechoslovakia and Bratislava in 1968

▲ Soviet tanks in Bratislava (**MAP** ★C9) crushed the dreams of freedom in 1968

At this time, Alexander Dubček, a liberal Slovak politician became the first secretary of the Communist Party. He started to carry out vast liberal reforms and the situation in Czechoslovakia was dramatically changed. In 1968, some of the conservative members of the Communist Party reached out to Moscow and asked for an intervention.

▼ Demonstration at SNP suqare (**MAP** ▲L4) in 1989. The communism fell a month later.

This liberal reform movement ended the night of August 20, 1968, when approximately 300,000 soldiers from the Soviet Union together with Bulgaria, East Germany, Hungary and Poland invaded Czechoslovakia.

▲ 109 people queueing in front of a butcher shop

The invasion put the conservative personalities in leading roles. This caused a new wave of purges, censorship and restrictions of freedom. The economy also suffered and the standard of living steadily declined.

VELVET REVOLUTION

In November 1989, Czechs and Slovaks became encouraged by the success of East Germany and other neighboring countries who started to shed the authoritarian rule. Series of demonstrations started on November 16, 1989 in Bratislava, Prague and Brno and eventually caused the dissolution of the Communist regime and the establishment of a new democratic rule.

PRACTICAL INFO

PARKING

Parking a car in the city-center is getting more difficult each year. While the streets were practically empty ten years ago, you can now drive for a good half an hour to find a spot on the street.

FREE PARKING

Street parking is very limited during workdays. However, you should be able to find free street parking within walking-distance of the city-center.

PAID STREET PARKING

Scratch-off parking cards can be bought from street vendors. These vendors are located in areas where paid street parking is available and they can be recognized by their reflective vests. € 0.8 per hour.

TOWING

The Bratislava city police do a surprisingly good job nowadays. Your vehicle will be towed or fitted with a boot for having parked illegally. Call (C) 159 to check if your vehicle was towed.

Private parking
Do not park unless outside of the specified time interval.

Paid parking
Buy a scratch-off card.

Free parking
Check for additional white signs.

TRAINS

Most trains depart from the Main Train Station (Slovak: Hlavná stanica) **MAP** ●3, but some trains to Vienna depart from Petržalka Train Station.

Purchase a ticket at the train station counter before you enter any train. When purchasing the ticket, state the destination and the type of train you intend to travel on.

PUBLIC TRANSPORTATION

Public transportation in Bratislava works relatively well and we encourage you to use it; especially if you want to experience daily life in Bratislava.

HOW TO TRAVEL

Tickets have to be purchased from newsstands or yellow ticket machines prior to boarding the vehicle. The machines only accept coins and are able to give change.

Mark the ticket in any marking machine as soon as you enter the vehicle.

VEHICLES

Bratislava's public transport system operates: buses, trams and trolley-busses. Most of the vehicles have LED displays showing the next stop.

▼ Mark your ticket after you enter the vehicle

▲ Yellow ticket machine

FARES

15 minutes (one ride only)	€ 0.70
60 minutes	€ 0.90
24 hours	€ 4.50
48 hours	€ 8.30
Three days	€ 10.00

POPULAR ROUTES

City-center - Petržalka Train Station
Take bus #93 from the Zochova bus stop. The Main Train Station is the terminal stop. (~6 min)

City-center - Devín castle
Take bus #29 from Nový Most bus stop. Devin Castle is the terminal stop. (~20 min)

City-center - Airport
Travel to the Main Train Station and then take bus #61. The airport is the terminal stop. (~21 min)

City-center - Petržalka Train Station
Take bus #80 from Zochova bus stop. Get off the bus at the ŽST Petržalka stop. You can recognize when to take off the bus when you see a modern train station building on the left-hand side. (~6 min)

TAXI

Taxis can be found waiting near taxi stands. However, it might be easier and often much cheaper to call for one in advance. If you are outside of the city-center, calling for a cab will be necessary. Most of the time, calling a cab will cost about half the price of those hailed on the street.

HOW TO CHOOSE

Taxis are not commissioned by the state or city. They are either signed with a taxi company or independent taxi drivers.

▲ Don't expect favorable exchange rates

When taking a taxi from the street, try to look for one with a company label. These tend to be safer and cheaper than unmarked cars.

PRICES

Always negotiate the fare in advance.

If you call a taxi in advance expect to pay approximately € 2.00 + € 0.60/km with minimum fare being € 3.50. You can expect to pay double for taking a taxi on the street.

PAYING

All taxis accept cash. If the taxi accepts payment cards, it has the logo stickers on the window. Leaving € 0.20 - € 0.50 tip is considered appropriate. Drivers will accept foreign currency, but don't expect the exchange rates to be favorable.

SMOKING

Be careful - some taxi drivers smoke. When you are making a phone order, ask for a non-smoker car.

SAMPLE FARES

Route	Call in	Taxi stand
Within the city-center	€ 3.00	€ 8.00
Main Train Station - City-center	€ 3.50	€ 11.00
Airport - City-center	€ 10.00	€ 25.00
Bratislava - Vienna Airport	€ 60.00	~ € 100.00

AIRPORT

▲ New terminal at Bratislava airport

M. R. Štefánik Airport or Bratislava Airport is located 9 km northeast of the Bratislava city-center. It is Slovakia's main international airport with annual passenger traffic of 1.7 million.

Scheduled and unscheduled domestic and international air connections are provided to destinations in Europe, the Middle East and North Africa.

DRIVING

Slovakia has over 18,000 kilometers of paved roads; 17% of which are 1st class roads. The road network is dense and fairly well-maintained.

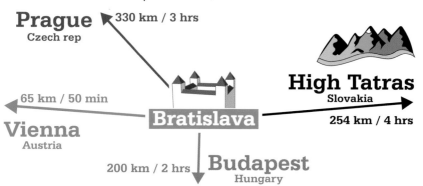

Prague ↖ **330 km / 3 hrs**
Czech rep

High Tatras
Slovakia

65 km / 50 min ←
254 km / 4 hrs →

Vienna
Austria

Bratislava

200 km / 2 hrs ↓ **Budapest**
Hungary

DRIVE ON THE <u>RIGHT</u>

Slovakia, like the rest of continental Europe, drives on right-hand side of the road, but it wasn't always like this. Cars drove on the left-side until the German occupation in 1938. This fact is often used to identify if a photo was taken before or after the World War II.

HEADLIGHTS

As of February 1, 2009, Slovak law requires drivers to have their headlights on all year long during the day and night.

TOLL ROADS

Vignettes are obligatory for all vehicles up to 3.5 tons which are passing along Slovak highways outside cities. Drivers without a valid vignette will be charged with cash fines between € 100 and € 500.

Vignettes can be purchased in almost every gas station and are offered in weekly, monthly or annual variants.

SCHENGEN AREA

Before Slovakia joined the Schengen Area in 2007, people traveling abroad often spent several hours waiting for the enthusiastic border officer to stamp their passports.

SPEED LIMITS

Town / Village	50 km/h
Outside of town / village	90 km/h
Highways	130 km/h
Highway in the city	90 km/h

ALCOHOL

The alcohol limit is 0.0%. This is very strict. If caught, expect to pay up to €1,300 in fines and face up to 1 year in prison.

PRICES

Slovakia joined the Eurozone on January 1, 2009 when the official currency changed from the Slovak koruna to the Euro (€).

Prices in Slovakia are, in general, lower than any other country in the European Union. Prices of imported items, such as electronics, are more or less the same as in the neighboring countries; whereas prices of products made in Slovakia are lower. Services are often considerably cheaper. This might mean it would not be a bad idea to get a haircut or visit a dentist here.

The average net income of a working person in Slovakia is around € 786 per month.

GROCERIES

Bread (1 kg)	€ 0.80
Milk (1.0 l)	€ 0.60
Bottled water (0.5 l)	€ 0.50
Chicken breasts (1 kg)	€ 6.00
Apples (1 kg)	€ 1.00
Eggs (10 pcs)	€ 1.20
Ham (1 kg)	€ 4.50

DINING

prices per adult

Hot dog	€ 0.80
Fast-food meal	€ 4.60
Casual restaurant	€ 6.00
Upscale restaurant	€ 12.00
Beer (0.5 l)	€ 1.50
Coffee	€ 1.50

SERVICES

Haircut (men)	€ 10.00
Haircut (women)	€ 25.00
Dentist examination	€ 30.00
Dentist filling	€ 50.00

ENTERTAINMENT

prices per adult

Cinema	€ 8.00
Theater	€ 13.00
Water park (3 hrs)	€ 12.00
Bowling (1 hr)	€ 20.00
Shooting range (1 hr)	€ 20.00
Golf (18 holes)	€ 50.00

ACCOMODATION

prices per night (if not specified otherwise)

Hostel	€ 13
3* Hotel	€ 55
4* Hotel	€ 85
Boutique Hotel	€ 175
Apartment (1 month)	€ 800
Apartment rent (long-term)	€ 500

OTHER

Petrol (1 l)	€ 1.50
Train to Vienna (return ticket)	€ 11
Air ticket to London	€ 80

CLIMATE

Bratislava is located inland and has the characteristic mild climate and four distinct seasons. Winters are cold and humid with temperatures averaging around -1°C. Spring and autumn are mostly sunny and windy with temperatures around 8 to 15 °C. Summers are warm and dry with average daily temperature high of 26 °C.

Bratislava has 116 rainy days per year, with yearly precipitation of 557 mm; which is about the same as London (601 mm), but slightly less than Paris (649 mm) or Rome (874 mm).

The longest day in Bratislava, the 21st of June, has 16 hrs, 04 min. The shortest, the 22nd of December, has only 8 hrs, 20 min.

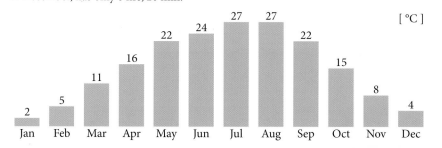

[°C]

Jan	Feb	Mar	Apr	May	Jun	Jul	Aug	Sep	Oct	Nov	Dec
2	5	11	16	22	24	27	27	22	15	8	4

WHEN TO VISIT

For those who have the luxury to decide when to travel, this section presents the highlights and drawbacks of the four seasons.

SUMMER

Summer is the most popular and arguably the best time to visit Bratislava.

➕ Some attractions are only open during the summertime (e.g., boat cruises)

➖ Hotel prices tend to be higher

▼ Winters in Bratislava are romantic

WINTER

Bratislava has a nice Christmas market in the Main Square which opens in late November and lasts until Christmas.

➕ Christmas atmosphere

➖ It might be too cold for sightseeing

➖ Attractions have shorter opening hours

AUTUMN

Visiting Bratislava in autumn is absolutely not a bad idea if you enjoy sightseeing.

➕ Temperatures stay comfortably warm and breezy

➕ Accommodation prices are lower than in summer

➖ The weather is not entirely predictable and it might get colder overnight; so pack warm clothes.

SPRING

Many argue that spring is the perfect time to visit Bratislava.

➕ Flowers everywhere

➕ Services tend to be better since it's the start of tourist season for locals.

➖ Few attractions remain closed until summer.

SLOVAK LANGUAGE

The Slovak language, or Slovenčina, is an Indo-European language. More specifically, it belongs to a group of West Slavic languages along with Czech and Polish. It's the only official language of Slovakia, where it's spoken by 5 million people. Most of the foreign speakers are in the United States (1,200,000) and Czech Republic (350,000).

One of the principles of Slovak spelling is the phonetic principle; meaning that words are written as they are heard, which makes it easy to write any word you hear.

CHARACTERS

Slovak uses the Latin alphabet with a few extra characters. These characters are comprised of regular Latin characters with one of four diacritics placed above. For example: á or č.

DIFFICULT?

Because of complex grammar rules, many exceptions and tricky pronunciation, the Slovak language is considered by many to be one of the hardest languages to learn.

▼ The High Tatras National Park is the pride of Slovakia

FIRST CONTACT

English	Slovak
Hello	Ahoj
Hello (Formal)	Dobrý deň
Goodbye	Dovidenia
How are you?	Ako sa máš?
Thank you	Ďakujem
My name is ...	Volám sa ...
I'm sorry	Prepáč
I don't speak Slovak	Nehovorím po Slovensky
Yes / No	Áno / Nie
Please	Prosím
Where / When / Who / How	Kde / Kedy / Kto / Ako
How do I get to the castle?	Ako sa dostanem na hrad
Prohibited	Zakázané

SERVICES

English	Slovak
Food	Jedlo
Drink	Pitie
Breakfast / Lunch / Dinner	Raňajky / Obed / Večera
Meat / Vegetables	Mäso / Zelenina
Hour / Day / Week / Month / Year	Hodina / Týždeň / Deň / Mesiac / Rok
Izba	Room
From / To	Od / Do
How much does it cost?	Koľko to stojí?
Open / Closed	Otvorené / Zatvorené
Entry / Exit	Vstup / Východ

EMERGENCIES

English	Slovak
Help	Pomoc
Fire	Oheň
Accident	Nehoda
Hospital	Nemocnica
Injury	Zranenie

ĽUDOVÍT ŠTÚR

Ľudovít Štúr was a Slovak: poet, journalist, publisher, teacher, linguist and politician. He was the chief figure of the Slovak national movement; which eventually standardized the Slovak language into its contemporary form.

Although, Štúr is often recognized as a national hero, some critics argue that the Slovak language could have been made more simple.

DAYS OF THE WEEK

Monday	Tuesday	Wednesday	Thursday	Friday	Saturday	Sunday
Pondelok	Utorok	Streda	Štvrtok	Piatok	Sobota	Nedeľa

COLORS

Červená	Zelená	Žltá	Modrá	Šedá	Biela	Čierna

NATIONAL HOLIDAYS

Slovakia has 15 days of public holidays, but most of the shops remain open according to Sunday's opening hours.

LIST OF PUBLIC HOLIDAYS

Date	Holiday
1 January (1993)	Day of the Establishment of the Slovak Republic
6 January	Epiphany
March, April	Good Friday
March, April	Easter Monday
1 May (1886)	International Workers' Day
8 May (1945)	Day of victory over fascism
5 July (863)	St. Cyril and Methodius Day
29 August (1944)	Slovak National Uprising anniversary
1 September (1992)	Day of the Constitution of the Slovak Republic
15 September	Day of Blessed Virgin Mary, patron saint of Slovakia
1 November	All Saints' Day
17 November (1989)	Beginning of the Velvet Revolution
24 December	Christmas Eve
25 December	Christmas Day
26 December	St. Stephen's Day

▼ Massive demonstrations in November 1989

HEALTH

EMERGENCIES

The all-encompassing emergency number is 112. When calling, state your emergency and where you are. If you are not sure of the exact address, try to describe features of the surrounding area.

Calling 112 is always free and possible from all types of phones.

▼ Green cross is a symbol of pharmacy

EMERGENCY ROOMS

If you require medical help during weekends, holidays or during the nighttime, you can visit one of the hospitals with 24/7 emergency rooms.

Strečnianska 13   (☏ +421 2 62250944
Ružinovská 10   (☏ +421 2 48279257
Limbová 1   (☏ +421 2 59542754

DRINKING WATER

Nearly all water is potable and safe to drink. If it is not, it will be clearly marked because people are not accustomed to non-potable water. Bratislava's tap water is often rated amongst the cleanest in the world.

TICK BITES

If you spend some time in a forest or rural area, you might get bitten by a tick. While often harmless, it might carry an infectious disease like tick-borne meningoencephalitis. Seek medical help if you feel dizzy after getting bitten.

PHARMACIES

Drugs are not sold at grocery stores or supermarkets. All medical items are sold at dedicated pharmacies. They are marked by a green cross as seen on the picture. Pharmacies can be found in most shopping malls.

DENTISTS

Slovakia is the perfect place to have a dental check-up because it might be cheaper and the dentist may be more qualified than the one you would otherwise visit at home.

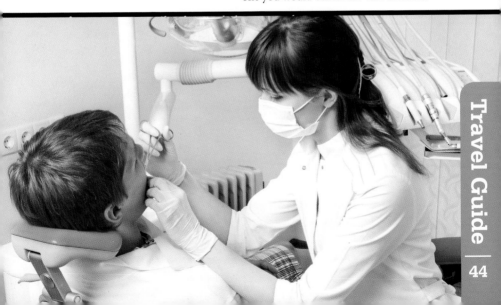

RANDOM TIPS

BUYING FLOWERS

When buying flowers, there is a simple rule. Flowers in even numbers are given only during funerals and odd numbers are given for every other occasion.

So buy 11 roses instead of a dozen.

VISITS

If you are invited to visit someone's home, take off your shoes when you come in. Do this even if the host is telling you not to. The host just wants to be polite, but doesn't re-

▲ When buying flowers, ask the florist for help. They don't like when you are touching the flowers.

ally want you walking around in your shoes.

HOMELESS

Don't give in to a homeless person begging for money. You might think you are doing a good deed, but really you are just keeping him on the street.

If you want to help, buy a homeless magazine titled, "Nota bene".

CRIME

Bratislava is a safe city; especially the city-center and its surroundings. There really aren't places you shouldn't go to.

The crime rate was at its highest after the revolution, but has decreased rapidly in last ten years.

WHEELCHAIRS

Bratislava is a memento of Communist attitude towards the disabled. Nothing built during the Communist era was wheelchair accessible.

After the revolution, a law was passed that new public buildings have to have wheelchair-accessible entries and many sidewalks were modified to accommodate the needs of wheelchair users.

CROSSING A ROAD

Roads should be crossed only in the marked pedestrian crossing. Pedestrians have priority over cars, so if there seems to be an endless stream of cars running, just step slowly onto the crossing and the next car will stop.

Although the same rule applies to all of Slovakia, you may need to be more careful when visiting cities other than Bratislava. In some regions, stepping onto the pedestrian crossing means nothing to oncoming drivers.

STAMPS

Stamps can always be purchased at post offices and sometimes in souvenir shops and newstands.

The post office is located at Námestie SNP (MAP ▲L4).

DATE FORMAT

Official date format is day.month.year. For example, 01.05.1995 is the 1st of May, 1995. Be careful if you come from a country that lists the month first and the day second as you could easily come a few months late or early.

OUTLETS

Slovakia uses a CEE 7/5 socket; which is Europlug compatible with 230 V plugs operating at 50 Hz. Child-resistant outlet shutters are not mandatory in Slovakia, so be careful.

TAKING PICTURES

Some of the sights don't allow pictures of the interior to be taken or there might be an extra charge for taking pictures. Try to look around and if you don't see the "Don't take pictures" sign, you are OK.

PHONES

The international prefix for Slovakia is +421 or 00421 and cell phones operate on GSM 900/1800.

Currently, there are three network carriers: Orange, T-mobile and O2 Telefonica. Each offers prepaid plans which can be bought either at their shop or at many other locations; including grocery stores.

COMMUNICATION

Not many people speak a language other than Slovak, so expect some difficulties if you try to use your native language. If you would like to ask something on the street, the rule of thumb is, the younger the person, the higher chance is that he or she will speak English.

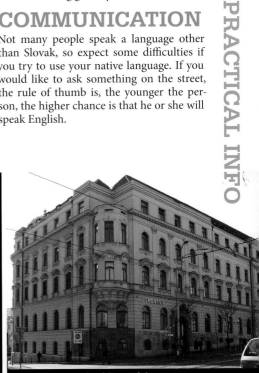

▲ Czechloslovak stamp printed in 1936 with a painting of Bratislava

▲ Art nouveau building of the main post office built in 1909.

▼ Watch out for trams. They have priority over pedestrians.

WHAT TO SEE

BRATISLAVA CASTLE

MAP ▲1 🕐 10:00 - 18:00 📞 +421 2 20483104 🌐 bratislava-hrad.sk

PREHISTORY

The Danube was so shallow near the castle hill that it could be crossed on foot; which made the location very attractive. This is why the castle hill was inhabited since approximately 3500 B.C. and several ancient trade routes crossed here.

CELTS AND ROMANS

The castle hill later became important for the Celts. A great number of Celtic coins

▲ Ruins of the Bratislava Castle in the late 18th century

were found here; indicating that there was also a mint. The coins are called "Biatec"; presumably after the king depicted on them.

The castle hill was at the border of the Roman Empire since 9 B.C. and was settled by Romans during the Roman period (1st to 4th century A.D.).

GREAT MORAVIA

Slavs, predecessors of present-day Slovaks, came to the castle hill around the year 500. At first they used older structures left by Celts and Romans with added fortification. In the 8th century a stone Slavic castle with wooden ramparts was constructed.

▼ The Castle with its present-day looks

MIDDLE AGES

The construction of a new stone castle began in the 10th century. This castle protected the Kingdom of Hungary against Bohemian (Czech) and German attacks.

In 1182 Friedrich Barbarossa gathered his crusader army near the castle. The troops then continued east on both sides of the Danube and used the river for transportation.

The well-fortified Bratislava Castle was among the few castles able to withstand Mongol attacks in 1241 and 1242.

KING SIGISMUND OF LUXEMBOURG

King Sigismund occupied the castle in 1385. He had ordered to improve fortifications to protect the castle against Hussite attacks. The wooden rampart was replaced by a stone defense wall. Expert engineers from Germany designed the largest castle ever built. To build this castle, taxes were increased and material was imported from around the kingdom. Unfortunately, the only preserved part left from these plans is the Sigismund Gate.

PRESSBURG AS CAPITAL

▼ Crown jewels of the Kingdom of Hungary

After the Kingdom of Hungary was defeated at the Battle of Mohács in 1526, during which the king died, the remaining royal family fled from Buda (Budapest) to Pressburg (Bratislava). Consequently, Bratislava Castle became the formal seat of kings of Royal Hungary and the crown jewels were kept in Bratislava's castle guarded by 50 Hungarian and 50 Austrian soldiers. The castle underwent several reconstructions; which included the addition of one floor and the rebuilding of two walls. Fortifications were also improved since the territory faced frequent Ottoman attacks.

MARIA THERESA

In 1740 Maria Theresa became the queen of the Kingdom of Hungary and promised the nobles she would spend time both in Austria and in the Kingdom of Hungary; to which Bratislava was the capital city. She converted Bratislava Castle from a defense-type castle to a proper royal residence. For example, she had the interior stairs rebuilt to a lower gradient so she could ride her own horse up them. Water delivery systems were constructed to deliver water from a tank in the lower-lying parts of town.

▲ Custom made for Maria Theresa so she could ride her horse up these stairs

▼ Castle's courtyard in 1953

DESTRUCTION

In 1783, the crown jewels were moved to Budapest and Bratislava Castle lost its importance. The castle's luxurious interior was rebuilt to serve as barracks. In 1809, the castle was bombarded by Napoleon cannons and in 1811 a fire set by an Austrian or Italian soldier destroyed most of the castle.

RECONSTRUCTION

The castle was reconstructed by volunteers without the support of the Communist government. The reconstruction started in 1955 and finished in 1968. The castle was recently reconstructed again with many changes including changing the wall color from brown to white.

▲ Vienna Gate

WHAT TO SEE

4 WEST WALL

It might seem that the castle has a square layout, but in fact, the West wall is the longest and the thickest since it was most likely to be bombarded. By making the wall the longest, it protected all three other sides. The wall is, on average, 7 meters thick with some places measuring up to 12 meters.

1 VIENNA GATE

Today's main entrance gate was built in 1712 for the coronation of Charles VI (father of Maria Theresa).

2 SVÄTOPLUK

The statue located directly in front of the castle represents Svätopluk, the king of Great Moravia, who lived from around 830 - 894. Although disputed by historians, he is regarded as the "King of Ancient Slovaks".

3 WEST TERRACE

A U-shaped building was built on a covered moat in front of West wing in 1764. This building was used for the stable and staff quarters.

▼ Statue of Svätopluk   ▼ Lugiland bastion

5 BAROQUE GARDENS

A large French garden in Schönbrunn-style was added to the northern part around 1750 by Emperor Francis I who was interested in botany. The garden was cascading and had oil lamps for night lighting. There was a plan to rebuild the gardens, but due

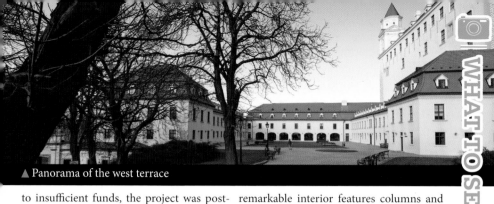

▲ Panorama of the west terrace

to insufficient funds, the project was postponed.

6 LUGINSLAND BASTION

A massive bastion was added in the 15th century to the already existing fortifications to keep enemies away from the area between the castle and the city. The bastion served as a heavy cannon post and also housed barracks. Luginsland is a German word meaning "guard tower".

7 SIGISMUND GATE

The southeast gothic entrance gate is the best preserved original part of the site. It was built in the 15th century by Sigismund of Hungary.

8 BAROQUE STABLE

The building originally built in the 18th century as a stable is one of the few structures that was not destroyed by the fire in 1811. Its

▼ The Sisigmund gate

▼ The baroque stable

remarkable interior features columns and arches and is now being used as a restaurant.

9 ST. ELISABETH

You may find a statue representing St. Elizabeth of Hungary who is thought to have been born in 1207 at Bratislava Castle. She was betrothed to Ludwig IV of Thuringia at the age of four and later married when she was fourteen. When she was twenty, her husband died of plague. She was canonized in 1235 for her charitable efforts.

10 LEOPOLD GATE

In connection with the Ottoman campaigns against Austria, military engineers designed complex fortification improvements. They designed star-shaped fortifications with bastions bet-

St. Elisabeth ▲

▲ Leopold gate

Travel Guide

52

ter suited to protect the castle against cannon fire. Fortification work stopped when Ottoman armies were stalled by the lost battle of Vienna in 1683 and only two bastions and the Leopold Gate had been built.

11 CROWN TOWER

A huge residential tower was constructed to protect the kingdom from Mongol attacks in 1245. The tower is the oldest preserved part of the castle and is the biggest of all four towers. Between the years 1552 and 1784, the Hungarian crown jewels were deposited in this tower. The top of the tower is open to the public and offers spectacular views of the city.

▼ The castle's towers might seem to be exactly the same, but the southwestern one is significantly larger

▲ Stones shows the floorplan of basilica from the 9th century

BASILICA

To the east of the castle are located illustrative ruins of the Great Moravian basilica (9th century), tower (10th century) and the Church of St. Savior (11th century); which were uncovered in 1965 with a great number of archeological findings. Debris from the Great Moravian basilica was found in the defense walls.

13 THERESIANUM

In 1765, Albert of Saxe-Teschen, Maria Theresa's son-in-law, came to live in the castle, but the castle's interior didn't provide enough space, so a new palace in the classic-style was built at the location of the eastern wall. The palace was expensively furnished and included hundreds of pieces of art. Theresianum was destroyed by fire in 1811.

14 ORATORY

The modern window on the east wall shows the remains of the oratory and chapel built in the 16th century. During the Baroque conversion, the oratory was walled up; which later preserved this part of castle. The oratory was discovered during the 20th century restorations.

▼ Theresianum: Maria Theresa built a baroque mansion right next to the castle so that the castle could serve as a summer-house

15 GOTHIC WINDOW

The original 16th century window can be seen on south wall of the castle. It was uncovered and partially reconstructed during the recent reconstruction of the castle.

16 WINNER'S GATE

During reign of Maria Theresa in the second half of the 18th century, a symmetrical courtyard was built in front of the castle's gate. Two

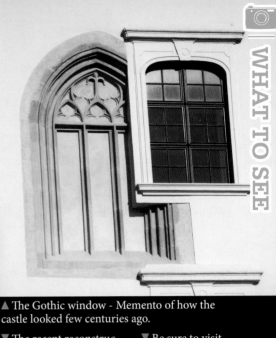

▲ Winners' gate

▼ This beautiful oratory is behind the modern glass window on the east side

▲ The Gothic window - Memento of how the castle looked few centuries ago.

▼ The recent reconstruction cost over € 50 million

▼ Be sure to visit the tower

▼ The interier is beautifully decorated thanks to the recent reconstruction

ST. MARTIN'S CATHEDRAL

MAP ▲2 🕐 9:00 - 16:00 📞 +421 2 54431359 🌐 dom.fara.sk € 2.00

St. Martin's Cathedral is the largest and one of the oldest churches in Bratislava. It is most known for being the coronation church of the Kingdom of Hungary.

Catholic Masses for the whole city originally took place at Bratislava Castle. This meant that a lot of people were crossing fortification gates of the castle to attend the worship several times a week. As the city grew, this became impractical and even served as a threat to the castle's safety. Because of this, a decision was made to relocate the Masses to the lower city. Soon after, the small church was insufficient and the construction of a new Gothic cathedral began in 1311. Due to several halts, the cathedral wasn't finished until 1452, when it was finally roofed and consecrated. The cathedral underwent several reconstructions, the addition of new structures, and finally received its present-day appearance in 1877 when it was reconstructed after damage was caused by fire and an earthquake.

1 TOWER

The 87-meter high tower was originally built for fortification purposes. It housed cannons and was part of the defense walls around the city. It was damaged by several fires caused by lightning and got its present-day appearance after Neo-Gothic reconstruction in 1849. Behind the clock is a bell-house with eight bells; of which, the heaviest and oldest is a 2,513 kg bell cast in 1675.

▲ Gold plated crown at the top weighs 300kg

2 CROWN

On the very top of the spire sits a cushion with a replica of the Crown of St. Stephen. It was installed during the 1835-1849 reconstruction. It weighs 300 kg, is over 1 meter in diameter and is gold-plated with 8 kg of gold.

3 PRESBYTERY

Presbytery is an area in church reserved for the clergy. Soon after the cathedral was finished in 1452, the presbytery proved to be too short. It was then demolished and built

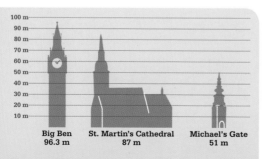

	Big Ben 96.3 m	St. Martin's Cathedral 87 m	Michael's Gate 51 m

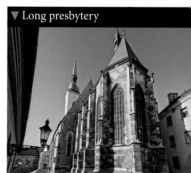

▼ Long presbytery

again, but this time was longer and more spacious and with expensive decor. The presbytery is Gothic with a typical rib-vault ceiling.

4 ST. ANNE CHAPEL

The St. Anne Chapel was built exactly over the original north entrance and is also called "the small portal". This portal can be seen from the inside and exhibits beautiful Gothic embellishment. The entrance to the catacombs is located in the chapel.

▲ North portal

5 NORTH PORTAL

The cathedral's present-day main entrance was built in the 15th century after building the St. Anne Chapel covered previous north entrance. Neo-Gothic lining can be seen on the door frame.

6 MEDIEVAL TOILET

The cathedral was originally part of the city's defense wall. The small tower on the northwest corner was not yet inside the city's wall. It was built in the 15th century and was used as a toilet with a moat under it.

7 ST. JOHN THE MERCIFUL CHAPEL

This Baroque chapel was designed by one of the most prolific Austrian sculptors, Georg Rafael Donner. It was built during the Baroque re-construction of the cathedral in first half of the 18th century. It serves as

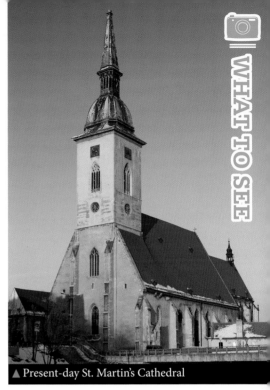
▲ Present-day St. Martin's Cathedral

a mausoleum of the 7th century saint, Saint John the Merciful, who lies here to this day.

8 UNFINISHED WINDOW

Notice the unfinished window at the south side of the cathedral approximately at eye-level. The reason why there is only half of a window is unclear.

▼ Medieval toilet   ▼ St. John the Merciful chapel

1 ORGAN

The organ loft was built according to the specifications of Ferenz Liszt; such that both the symphonic orchestra and the choir could fit there. The previous organ, built in 1880, was replaced in 2010 by a brand-new organ built by Gerald Woehl.

▲ Brand new pipe Organ

The new organ has over 4,500 pipes. The smallest is 5 millimeters and the largest is 10 meters high. Several experts have said that the sound of the new organ is exceptional. Thus, if you have a chance, listen to the sound of the € 1 million instrument.

2 ALTAR OF BLESSED VIRGIN MARY

This altar, built around 1642, features a central statue of Mary with Jesus and several surrounding statues of saints and a depiction of the burial of Jesus.

3 SAINT MARTIN WITH A BEGGAR

A valued Baroque Equestrian statue of St. Martin is located in the corner of the right nave. It was made by Rafael Donner in 1735 and depicts St. Martin sharing his coat with a beggar. Notice the Baptismal font dated 1409 with the Neo-

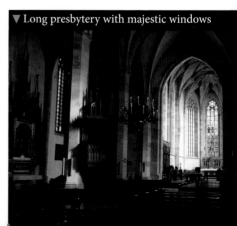

▼ St. Martin sharing his coat with a beggar

▼ Altar of the Blessed Virgin Mary

▼ St. John the Merciful Chapel

Gothic upper portion dated 1878.

4 ST. JOHN THE MERCIFUL CHAPEL

The interior decor of the chapel is a showcase of works of Viennese High Baroque. The relic remains of St. John the Merciful are preserved in the silver coffin under the golden drapes.

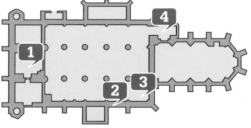

▼ Long presbytery with majestic windows

CORONATIONS

St. Martin's Cathedral was a coronation cathedral of the Kingdom of Hungary between the years 1563 and 1830.

During the 15th and 16th centuries, the Ottoman Empire raided southeastern Europe. After the Battle of Mohacs in 1526, the Ottoman Empire occupied most of the southern land of the Kingdom of Hungary. This made Bratislava the new capital city of the kingdom; placing it among other coronation cities.

The coronation process was very complex and had many customs. The celebration often lasted several days. In total, ten kings, one queen and eight of their consorts had been coronated here.

Since 2003, there has been an annual cultural event called the "Coronation celebration"; which reenacts the coronation process.

▼ St. Martin's Cathedral in around 1760

LIST OF CORONATIONS

Maximillian II
8 September 1563

Maria (♥ Maximilian II)
9 September 1563

Rudolf II
25 September 1572

Matthias
19 November 1608

Anna (♥ Matthias)
25 March 1613

Ferdinand II
1 July 1618

Eleonore (♥ Ferdinand II)
26 July 1622

Maria Anna (♥ Ferdinand III)
14 February 1638

Ferdinand IV
16 June 1647

Eleanor (♥ Ferdinand III)
6 June 1655

Leopold I
27 June 1655

Joseph I
9 December 1687

Charles III
22 May 1712

Elisabeth Christine (♥ Charles III)
18 October 1714

Maria Theresa
25 June 1741

Leopold II
15 November 1790

Maria Ludovika (♥ Francis I)
7 September 1808

Caroline Augusta (♥ Francis I)
25 September 1825

Ferdinand V
28 September 1830

MAIN SQUARE

MAP ▲3

Slovak: Hlavné námestie. The best known square in Bratislava; often considered to be the very center of the city.

HISTORY

The earliest documents to mention the Main Square date back to the 14th century. While the square is now used mainly to enjoy pleasant summer days, in the past it was used for everything except rest. In addition to markets, the square was also used for various assemblies, celebrations and it was also a place where executions took place. To accommodate these requirements, the square was much larger than the present-day square. Another difference is that while the square is rectangular now, it was more of a round shape in the 14th century.

The most important building is the **1** **Old Town Hall** (📄 61).

▲ Maximillian fountain

2 MAXIMILLIAN FOUNTAIN

This fountain was built in 1572 by the first king coronated in Bratislava, Maximillian II. During the coronation celebrations a firework started a fire that destroyed part of the city. One of the reasons this fire was not extinguished effectively was the lack of water. To prevent this from ever happening again, King Maximillian II built a large fountain. His statue is situated on top. This fountain is the oldest and probably the most known in Bratislava.

3 GAS LIGHTING

The Main Square was one of the first public places to have gas lighting in Bratislava. The gas lighting was placed here around 1856 to provide light to the marketplace and was later removed by the end of the 19th century when the square was converted into a park. Although the original gas lighting did not persevere, historians successfully identified its appearance and location and a replica has been put in place during a recent reconstruction.

4 FRENCH SOLDIER STATUE

You can read more about the statue of the French soldier on page 📄 85. Two other bronze statues are nearby: Čumil (MAP ▲18) and Schöne Naci (MAP ▲K7).

5 PALUGYAY HOUSE

The site was originally occupied by a medieval house called the "Burg". This house was the tallest of all buildings on the Main Square and many of Bratislava's residents believe this house was the oldest in Bratislava and that Bratislava received its name "Pressburg" from this house. As with most old houses there is a legend that this house was haunted. It was eventually bought by a successful wine merchant, František Palugyay, who tore the "Burg" down and in 1882 built a Neo-Gothic house in its place.

6 GREEN HOUSE

The Green House, Zelený dom in Slovak, housed the state parliament and county council meetings. The house; which was built around the 14th century, was originally a residential house. Through time, there was a court, an inn and even a theater here; the latter of which was visited by Maria Theresa. The name might imply that it was painted green, but interestingly it was impossible to manufacture outdoor green paint until the second half of the 19th century. The house was named because it featured green paintings inside.

7 JESENÁK PALACE

Built in first half of the 18th century for Hungarian Baron Ján Jeszenák, it lies over the Gothic foundation of a previous building. The building had a waterproof room; probably used as a vault. It also had three fountains and a hole for ice storage. Jar fragments dating back to the 14th century have been found 4 meters below street-level. Július Mayer opened his Kaffee Mayer in 1913; which was reopened in 1997.

8 KUTSCHERFELD PALACE

Kutscherfeld Palace is the smallest Rococo palace in Bratislava. It was built in 1762 by Leopold von Kutscherfeld. Anton Rubinstein, a famous Russian pianist, composer and conductor lived in this housed briefly in 1847. Today, the building serves as the French Embassy.

▲ French soldier

▼ Main Square - Maximillian fountain, Palugyay house, Green house and Kutscherfeld palace. Photo was taken from the Jesenák palace

OLD TOWN HALL

MAP ▲4 📄 91

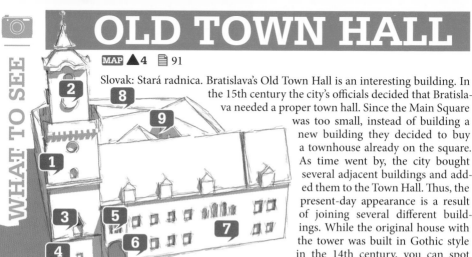

Slovak: Stará radnica. Bratislava's Old Town Hall is an interesting building. In the 15th century the city's officials decided that Bratislava needed a proper town hall. Since the Main Square was too small, instead of building a new building they decided to buy a townhouse already on the square. As time went by, the city bought several adjacent buildings and added them to the Town Hall. Thus, the present-day appearance is a result of joining several different buildings. While the original house with the tower was built in Gothic style in the 14th century, you can spot Renaissance and Baroque features as a result of multiple reconstructions.

1 TOWER

If you were rich in the 14th century, having a stone tower next to your house was always a good idea. It provided additional safety in case of a siege on the city and it also served as a fireproof storage space. This tower was built in the 13th or 14th century and is considered to be one of the oldest structures in the city.

▼ Clock

2 CLOCK

The tower housed a mechanical clock from the time it was built. The pocket watch was not created until the 16th century, and even then it was far too expensive to own and so public clocks together with church bells were the only way of telling time for majority of citizens. In the 16th century, a gold-plated globe showing the moon's phases was added under the clock.

3 CANNONBALL

In June 1809, Napoleon's army bombarded Bratislava from the south bank of the Danube. The siege caused significant damage to the city, but the bridge was successfully

▲ Cannonball lodged in a wall - Memento of a Napoleon's siege

defended. A few more buildings in the city still have cannonballs lodged in the walls.

4 FLOOD LINE

To this day, the most catastrophic flooding was on February 5, 1850. The Danube's river bed was blocked by ice and therefore the flood waves poured into the city. The height of the water on that day is represented by a flood mark.

5 BAY WINDOW

The bay window was added during the 16th century reconstruction. Originally built in Renaissance style, it received its present-day appearance in the 19th century. Notice the colorfully glazed roof tiles. There is a painting of a man to the left. It is unclear who he was and why his portrait is on the building.

6 PASSAGE

The passage into the courtyard features beautiful stone portals and is topped by a Gothic cross-ribbed vault with relief bolts. It was built in 1457 and retained its appearance to the present day.

7 PAWER'S HOUSE

One of the most most visible signs that the Town Hall is a result of joining multiple buildings is the Pawer House. It was built by a wealthy citizen, Hans Pawer, in 1422, but was purchased by the city and annexed to the Town Hall soon after in 1430. The recent reconstruction partially restored the facade.

▲ The Old Town Hall from the back side

8 EAST WING

The east wing was built in 1912; making it the newest part of the Old Town Hall. It has a Neo-Renaissance facade and the roof is covered by beautifully glazed roof tiles.

9 COURT-YARD

This courtyard is unique because it is formed by several buildings; each built in a different century. Notice the Gothic windows in the north wing. The arcade on the north and east side was added in the 20th century.

▲ The Old Town Hall is like a jigsaw puzzle with houses as pieces

▼ Colorful tiles on the bay window

PRIMATE'S PALACE

MAP ▲5

Slovak: Primaciálny palác. When Bratislava was the Capital city of the Kingdom of Hungary, Archbishop József Batthyány wanted to have a decent residence there. He hired a talented architect, Melchior Hefele, who had designed the most expensive and luxurious palace in Bratislava. It was built between 1777 and 1781 in Neo-Classical style. In addition to being the archbishop's winter residence, it was where the king's to-be slept the day before the coronation. The city bought the palace in 1903 and has used it as the Town Hall ever since. The palace is considered to be the most luxurious in Bratislava and features many ostentatiously decorated rooms; including the Hall of Mirrors and five colored lounges (green, brown, blue, red and gold).

▼ Putti - Baby statues

3 HUGE HAT

Notice the oversized hat over the tympanum. The hat is 180 cm in diameter and weights 150 kg. It is a cardinal's hat and should commemorate the palace's mission. Under the hat, we can see the family coat of arms of Archbishop Batthyány.

▲ Tympanum

1 PUTTI

Putti are figures of a human baby or toddler which are often found in Christian art. Notice the two letters "C" and "I" which represent the Archbishop's motto "Clementia et Iustitia" meaning "kindness and justice".

2 TYMPANUM

This Tympanum carries distinctive Neo-Classical features. The original fresco by Franz Anton Maulbertsch was severely damaged and had to be replaced in 1956 by Ernest Zmeták's stone mosaic which we see there today.

4 ST. GEORGE FOUNTAIN

Inside the courtyard, you will find a 17th century statue of St. George. He was a Roman soldier who lived in the 3rd century. According to a legend, one city had to offer a maiden every day to a dragon so that the dragon would allow for a spring that would provide water for the whole city. When random selection picked the princess, St. George came and killed the dragon, sav-

bought only the palace without any type of furnishing. In the end, the judge decided that the wallpaper and everything behind it was not considered furnishings and denied their complaint. The tapestries tell an ancient story of love and are on display on the first floor of the Palace.

6 THE HALL OF MIRRORS

The palace and its most famous chamber, the Hall of Mirrors, have been the host to many significant events. In 1805, Napoleon Bonaparte decisively won the Battle of Austerlitz against the Austrian Empire. As a result, 22 days later a peace treaty was signed in Bratislava's Hall of Mirrors. Large mirrors were among the most expensive luxury goods in the 18th century and people were amused by having a lot of them in one room. Today, it is used primarily as a concert room.

▼ St George killing a dragon

7 ST. LADISLAV CHAPEL

This unique oval-shaped chapel extends through all of the Palace's floors and is accessible from each of them. A mural on the central vault depicts the miracle of St. Ladislav, the Hungarian king. It is unclear who the author of the mural is, but some believe it was Franz Anton Maulbertsch. Notice the 18th century carved benches. The chapel is accessible only during Sunday mass.

▲ One of the valuable gobelins found during a reconstruction

▼ Spectacular interior

ing the princess along the way. The grateful citizens abandon their paganism and converted to Christianity.

Statues depicting him killing the dragon can be found all over Europe.

5 TAPESTRIES

When the city bought the Palace from the archbishopric and started reconstruction work, the tapestries were found hidden behind the wallpaper. These tapestries were woven around 1630 at the royal weaving workshop in Mortlake near London. They were professionally valued at 120,000 gold coins; which was exactly what the city had paid for the whole palace. The Esztergom canonry immediately pointed out that according to the contract of sale, the city

JÓZSEF BATTHYÁNY

József Batthyány was born in Vienna in 1729 to an old distinguished Hungarian family. He himself bore the title of count. At the age of 32, he was appointed to bishop and a year later to archbishop. He served as an advisor for both Maria Theresa and Joseph II, and coronated two kings in Bratislava.

MICHAEL'S GATE

MAP ▲6 🕐 10:00 - 17:00 📞 +421 2 54433044 🔗 muzeum.bratislava.sk 💶 4.30

Slovak: Michalská brána. Bratislava's fortification system was built in the 13th century. It included two rings of city walls, several bastions and three gates leading to the town; Michael's Gate (north), Vydrica Gate (west) and Laurinc Gate (east). In the 15th century another smaller gate, Fishermen's Gate (south), was added. Of these four gates, Michael's Gate is the only one remaining. On the sixth floor of the tower there is an observation deck that offers a magnificent view of the Old City, the castle, and surrounding areas. This deck is only accessible after purchasing a ticket to the Museum of Arms (📄 91).

1 NAME

The gate was named after St. Michael's church; which was directly in front of the gate in the 13th-14th century when the gate was built. In the 16th century, when the danger of being attacked by the Ottoman Empire was imminent, the church, along with other buildings, was demolished and the material was used to strengthen the defense structures.

2 TOMBSTONE

The only remainder of the outskirts which were in front of Michael's Gate is a pink tombstone built into the tower. The tombstone is visible from Michalská Street and is in the lower part of the left-hand corner where the tower meets the adjacent building.

▼ Tombstone from the original village

3 TOWER

The original tower was built in the 14th century along with the whole fortification system. The octagonal segment was added from 1511-1517. It received its present-day appearance during the 1753-1758 Baroque conversion. The tower has seven floors and is 51 meters high.

4 BARBICAN

Barbican is derived from Arabic or Persian and means "gate-house". It was a common practice to build an additional fortified outpost just outside of an existing gate to make the gate less vulnerable in the event of an attack. The barbican in front of the Michael's gate was built in the 15th century and although it is still there, it is not clearly visible because of the obstruction by newer buildings. Notice that the barbican still has openings that were used by ropes of a drawbridge.

5 MOAT

As in every decent city, Bratislava also had a moat in front of the city walls. The moat would make siege weapons, such as siege towers or battering rams, impossible to use and if filled with water, it made digging a tunnel under the wall very

▼ The barbican

▲ One of the narrowest houses in Europe at only 1.3 meters

difficult. The moat in front of Michael's Gate was, however, only a dry moat.

6 BRIDGE

The fortification in front of St. Michael's Gate was closed-off by a drawbridge over the moat. The entrance was closed by a drawn portcullis along with a wooden door. The wooden drawbridge was replaced by the present-day stone bridge in the end of the 18th century.

7 NARROW HOUSE

Adjacent to Michael's Gate is the narrowest house in Bratislava. It is only 1.3 meters wide; which is identical with the width of its door. In the 18th century, with the improvement in siege tactics and artillery, city walls became obsolete and an order was given by Maria Theresa to demolish the walls so that the city could expand faster. Removing the thick fortification wall created a gap which was eventually used to build this house. According to some, this is the narrowest house in Europe.

8 STATUE OF ST. MICHAEL

A statue of Archangel Michael slaying a dragon was placed on top of the tower during the Baroque conversion in 1753-1758. The popular motif represents the archangel fighting with the devil as mentioned in the

Book of Revelation. There is another statue of Archangel Michael on the bridge leading from the barbican of Michael's Tower.

9 CRESTS

There are two crests on Michael's Gate. The Gothic stone crest above the north entrance was placed there during reconstruction in the 16th century. The plaque on the outer side is cast from lead and was placed there during a Gothic conversion in the 18th century.

10 COMPASS ROSE

As a result of the city's recent initiative, a compass rose was added to the sidewalk passing by Michael's Gate. It shows distances and bearings to 29 world cities. The compass rose marks "Kilometer Zero", meaning distances to-and-from the city are measured from this point.

▼ Compass rose shows distances and bearings to 29 world cities

OPERA HOUSE

MAP ▲7 📄 95

Bratislava's first dedicated theater building was built in 1776. A few years later, in 1881, a fire at the Ring Theater in Vienna killed 620 people and left hundreds wounded. It was the deadliest single-building fire in history. This raised awareness about fire safety in public entertainment buildings all

▲ Ganymedes' fountain

over the world and forced Bratislava's officials to demolish the original, unsafe theater. The present-day opera house was built soon after and follows the design of Viennese architects F. Fellner and H. Helmer, who have built over 45 theater buildings across Europe. The building process took only two years and the Neo-Renaissance building was finished in 1886. The new building was built from strong fire-resistant materials and had fire hydrants connected to a water distribution system.

▲ Boy riding an eagle - scene from a story of Ganymedes

1 GANYMEDES' FOUNTAIN

The Neo-Baroque Fountain was designed and built by local artist, Viktor Tilgner, the creator of the Wolfgang Amadeus Mozart memorial in Vienna. The fountain depicts the Greek mythology tale of Ganymedes. Ganymedes was, according to Homer, the most beautiful of mortals which led the God Zeus to abduct him in the form of an eagle to serve him in Olympus. Four boys carry the four most abundant species of fish in the Danube. This fountain was the first fountain in Bratislava and was built solely for decorative purposes.

2 OPERA

Opera is part of Western classical music tradition in which singers and musicians perform a dramatic work combining text and musical score. Opera has roots in 16th century Italy, but quickly spread through the rest of Europe. Although Italian opera dominated, today's most renowned artist of the late 18th century opera is Mozart with pieces like, "The Marriage of Figaro" or "The Magic Flute".

3 HISTORY OF PERFORMING

The performances in this building were exclusively in German or Hungarian and were performed by touring ensembles. It was not until 1920 that the Slovak National Theater became housed here and still the Slovak National Theater had been run by Czech artists until 1938. In 1955, the drama ensemble was moved to a different building, leaving this building to opera and ballet ensembles.

4 INTERIOR

If you have a chance to go see one of the

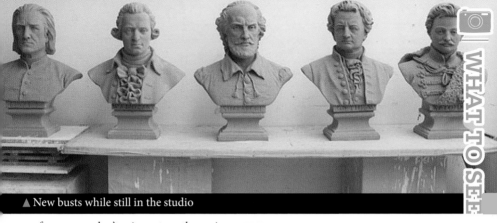

▲ New busts while still in the studio

performances, don't miss out on the majestic interior. The original Stucco and Fresco decoration can be seen in the lobby, stairways, first floor saloon, loggia and partially in the theater hall. Notice the original ceiling paintings by Munich artist Leo Lüttgendorf-Leinburg. When built, the theater, with 1,200 seats, was lit by 800 gas lamps and an electrical chandelier.

5 THE ARCHITECTS

Ferdinand Fellner and Hermann Helmer were indisputably two of the most influential theater architects in Europe. They built a total of 48 theaters in Europe. Because of their reliability, predictability and professionalism, they practically created a monopoly status in Austria-Hungary. The company was founded in 1873 by two classmates. In the first years, Fellner was responsible for the construction progress and negotiations; while Helmer worked in the office. Later, the contracts were divided and each architect had his own staff. They employed up to 20 architects.

6 BUSTS

Notice five busts in the oval niches on the front facade. They were originally placed there in 1886, but in 1934 the city governance could not bear the fact that the busts depicted Hungarian and Austrian artists and therefore had the busts removed. Their replicas were created and placed in the original location in 2003. The original bust of Mihály Vörösmarty did not persevere and had to be replaced by a bust of Wolfgang Amadeus Mozart. From left to right, the busts represent: Johann Wolfgang von Goethe, William Shakespeare, Wolfgang Amadeus Mozart, Franz Liszt and József Katona.

▲ Poster from 1920

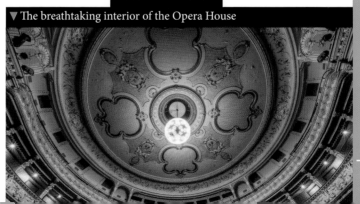

▼ The breathtaking interior of the Opera House

NEW BRIDGE

MAP ◆ 1 🕐 10:00 - 23:00

📞 +421 2 62520300 📱 u-f-o.sk 💶 € 5-7

New Bridge was formerly known as, "The Bridge of the Slovak National Uprising" (Slovak: "Most SNP"), and was later re-named, after the fall of Communism in Slovakia, to "New Bridge" (Slovak: "Nový most"). Don't let the name confuse you. This bridge is not new nor is it the newest. It is the second oldest with only the Old Bridge predating it. The New Bridge is the longest bridge in the world with one pylon and one cable-stayed plane, but the most interesting and the saddest thing is that a large part of the historical city-center had to be demolished to make room for the bridge's access road.

FACT SHEET

Construction start	1967
Construction end	1972
Total length	430,8 m
Longest span	303 m
Width	21 m
Total height	95 m
Number of lanes	4
Material	Steel

▲ View of the New Bridge from the Castle ▼ The New Bridge being built in 1971

1 CONTEXT

Before this bridge was built, Bratislava had only one bridge; the Old bridge, which connected Bratislava and Petržalka. When it was decided that a huge urban district would be built in Petržalka it became clear that an additional bridge would be needed.

2 LOCATION

The location of this bridge is probably the most controversial issue in Bratislava. Why it was chosen to build a bridge going directly into Bratislava's historical center remains hardly understandable to this very day. The fact that three more bridges have since been built proves that this was not the only possible location.

3 CONSTRUCTION

An international architectural design competition had been held for Bratislava's second bridge. The chosen design placed fourth, but due to economic reasons the first three designs were later dismissed. The construction of the bridge started in 1967 and the bridge was finished in 1972. An error in static calculations was found during constructions which required an additional brace to be placed on the left bank.

4 DEMOLITION

To make room for the road system leading from the bridge, the Communist Regime demolished approximately 380 buildings; including a synagogue adjacent to St. Martin's Cathedral. Most of the demolished buildings belonged to the Jewish population. The four-lane access road separates the castle and the historical center; which significantly disrupts Bratislava's historical atmosphere.

5 SYNAGOGUE

The Jewish population in Bratislava grew mostly during the second half of the 19th century due to immigration. The Neolog reform movement built a Moorish-style (Arabic influence) synagogue in 1893. The synagogue was rarely used after WWII and was gradually demolished by the city. Existence of a synagogue so close to a Catholic church is quite unique.

6 BRIDGE'S DESIGN

The bridge has one pylon consisting of two pillars and has one cable-stayed plane. The design of the bridge is interesting because the pylon is tilted to support the entire bridge so that no pillars are obstructing the river's flow. There are four car-lanes and two sidewalks for pedestrians and bicyclists. The bridge also houses a water pipe which supplies the historical center with water from Petržalka.

7 PYLON

The pylon is 85 m high and consists of two pillars; which meet at the top. A flying saucer-shaped structure housing a restaurant rests atop the pylon. There is also an observation deck at the very top. Of the two pillars, the left has an elevator and the right has an emergency staircase with 430 steep steps.

8 UFO

The restaurant at the top was reconstructed in 2005 and given the name "UFO". Along with a spectacular view, this restaurant offers one of the finest dining experiences in the city, but it's rather expensive so be prepared.

▲ Demolition works in 1969

▼ Detail of the UFO. What's inside? A restaurant.

OBSERVATION DECK

The observation deck is accessible by an elevator and offers one of the best views of the city.

FRANCISCAN CHURCH

MAP ▲8

The Franciscan Church is the oldest sacral building in Bratislava. The construction lasted 17 years, until it was finally consecrated in 1297 by the King of Hungary, Andrew III. While it was originally built in Gothic style, it was converted several times. The first of which was to a Renaissance style in the 17th century and then to Baroque style in the 18th century. When Bratislava was the coronation city of the Kingdom of Hungary from 1563-1830, each time a new king was being coronated in St. Martin's Cathedral, chosen nobles walked to the Franciscan Church and were knighted as Knights of the Golden Spur, the second highest catholic order. Throughout the centuries, the church had been damaged several times and only a small part of the original form is preserved.

▲ The Franciscan Church - The tower, pressbytery and part of the Chapel of St. John the Evangelist.

1 TOWER

The original Gothic hexagon tower was built in the 15th century. The bell in this tower rang in the morning to notify citizens that the local pubs were being opened, and then again in the evening to announce their closure. The original tower was the only part excluded from the multiple conversions and therefore kept its original appearance. Unfortunately, it was severely damaged during the 1897 earthquake. It was carefully lowered from the church and transported to one of the city parks, Sad Janka Kráľa (📄 79), and is still there today.

2 RELIC

The church houses a rare relic, the body of Saint Reparat. He was a passionate deacon in the city of Nola near Neapoli, Italy. He died as a Christian martyr in 353 and was buried in Rome. In 1769, his remains were exhumed and moved to Bratislava. The relic is on display in a decorative shrine in the main nave.

▼ The relic in the Franciscan church - Body of St. Reparat

4 ST. JOHN THE EVANGELIST CHAPEL

The Chapel of Saint John the Evangelist is considered one of the most significant works of Gothic architecture in Slovakia. It was built in the second half of the 14th century, when it replaced an older chapel that had been built in 1296. The chapel was built by the then-mayor Jakub to serve as his family's crypt. The chapel is praised for its timeless construction, high ceiling and beautiful vaults. The chapel had undergone reconstruction in 1831 when, along with others, a Neo-Classical pillared altar of

▲ The original tower was replaced by a replica after an earthquake in 1897.

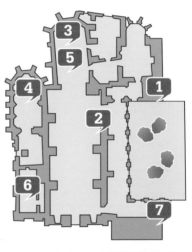

3 MAIN ALTAR

Most of the interior was replaced in the first half of the 18th century. The brick construction of the main altar was built in the years spanning from 1720-1730. The glass painting depicting the Annunciation is from the end of the 19th century. The altar is symmetrically flanked by the statues of Saint Stephan and Saint Emeric.

▼ Interior of the church with the Main Altar in the middle

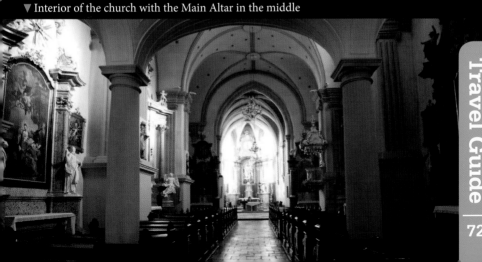

Saint John the evangelist was added.

5 PRESBYTERY

The presbytery is the only part of the church that has more or less retained its appearance throughout the centuries. Its exterior with high Gothic windows can be seen if you walk around the church.

7 MONASTERY

The Franciscan Monastery was the first in existence to be mentioned in the year 1273 when women used it as a shelter during the

▲ Original tower damaged in an earth-quake

Front facade ▲

6 LORETO CHAPEL

According to legend, when the house where the Virgin Mary lived came under threat during the turmoil of the Crusades, it was miraculously transported from Nazareth to present-day Croatia in 1291. After this location proved to be unsafe, it was transported yet again in 1294, and this time to Loreto, a small coastal city in Italy. A large basilica was later built over this house.

Because of this legend, multiple Loreto chapels were built around the world which resemble the original house in Loreto, Italy. The one in the Franciscan church was built in P1708 by an influential Palatine, Pavol Esterházy.

siege of Přemysl Otakar's armies in Bratislava. During the centuries, it was reconstructed several times. The city council meetings took place in the monastery's spacious halls. Today, it is being used by the Franciscan Order.

VISITING THE CHURCH

The church is open daily during the summer months to the public. During the other months, you can visit this church 30 minutes before mass.

MAP ▲ 8 📅 Jul - Aug 🕐 10:30 - 17:00
📞 +421 2 54432145 🔖 frantiskani.sk
€ Free

FRANCISCAN ORDER

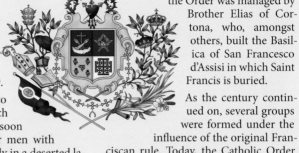

The most prominent of the Franciscans is the Order of Friars Minor, a Catholic religious order formed by Francis of Assisi in 1209.

In 1209, Francis began to live in poverty and preach repentance. He was soon joined by several other men with whom he lived ascetically in a deserted lazar-house near Assissi and traveled with through the neighboring country. Their lifestyle didn't go unnoticed and Francis soon got an audience with the Pope Innocent III., who ordained him as a deacon, allowing him to read the Gospel in church.

Transformation from the brotherhood to a full-scale order proved to be very difficult and time-consuming. Francis eventually resigned from the day-to-day operations, but retained his position in the Order.

After the death of Francis in 1226, the Order was managed by Brother Elias of Cortona, who, amongst others, built the Basilica of San Francesco d'Assisi in which Saint Francis is buried.

As the century continued on, several groups were formed under the influence of the original Franciscan rule. Today, the Catholic Order of Friars Minor comprises three separate groups: the Observants, the Capuchins and the Conventual Franciscans.

POOR CLARES

Parallel to the creation of the brotherhood by Francis of Assissi, a second Franciscan Order, the Poor Clares, was established. This order was founded by Clare of Assisi who was, at the age of 18, inspired by Francis's preaching at the cathedral.

Portrait of Saint ▲
Francis of Assissi

Basilica of San Francesco d'Assisi, Italy ▲

▲ Modern Franciscan

YOU MIGHT LIKE

CHURCHES

Similar to other European cities, sacral architecture makes for a large part of the historical buildings in the city. While other buildings were torn down when they were damaged, churches were rarely replaced by a non-sacral building. The preserved churches in Bratislava are in the Gothic, Renaissance, Baroque, Art Nouveau and Neoclassical architectural styles. The oldest church in Bratislava is the Franciscan Church, consecrated in 1297. The largest is St. Martin's Cathedral.

▲ The art nouveau Blue Church

1 BLUE CHURCH

Located east of the city-center is an Art Nouveau church formally known as the Church of St. Elizabeth. It was built in 1909-1913 according to the designs of Ödön Lechner, who designed a neighboring school building. The church was originally part of this school and served as the school's chapel. The church has one oval nave. The cylindrical tower is 36.8 m tall.

Notice the glazed roof tiles and heavy decoration. The church is very popular for weddings and Saturdays are often booked months in advance.

MAP ⭐1

2 ST. STEPHEN'S CHURCH

The Order of Capuchins came to Bratislava in 1676 from Vienna. Their first church was the Chapel of St. Catherine on Michalská Street. They bought the land where the church stands today in 1698 and built the monastery and a church by 1711. The church underwent several reconstructions and received its present-day appearance in 1860. The church has a vast system of catacombs with prominent people buried within them. A part of the catacombs has collapsed and neither the entrance nor the identities of the bodies are known.

The architecture corresponds with the principles of the Capuchins. Notice there isn't a tower and the church has stark lines with smooth, unadorned walls.

MAP ▲9

3 TRINITARIAN CHURCH

The Trinitarian Order started the construction of the church in 1717. It was sanctified in 1727, although work in the interior continued until the first half of the 18th century. The interior features an interesting cupola with a trompe l'oeil fresco. Trompe l'oeil (French for 'deceive the eye') uses realistic imagery in order to create an optical illusion that depicts objects as three-dimensional. In this case, it is seen from inside a huge dome.

MAP ▲10

▼ St. Stephen's Church

▲ Trinitarian Church

4 CHURCH OF THE POOR CLARES

The Gothic church and monastery were built in the 14th century by the Order of the Poor Clares. The Clares had to leave this church in 1782 after Joseph II, son of Maria Theresa, dissolved the Order. The church is now owned by the city and is being used as a concert hall thanks to its exceptional acoustics. One interesting feature is the pentaprism tower; which is quite unusual for a Gothic church.

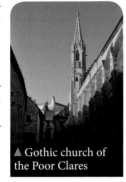
▲ Gothic church of the Poor Clares

MAP ▲ 11

5 SYNAGOGUE

Before World War II, there were three synagogues and the Jewish population comprised 10% of Bratislava's population. The two synagogues near the castle were demolished during the Communist Regime and now only around 800 Jews live in Bratislava (less than 0.2%). The only synagogue left was built in 1926 and was the only building on the street at that time.

MAP ▲ 12

▲ The now orthodox church of St. Nicholas' overlooking the city

6 CHURCH OF ST. NIKOLAJ

The church is located on the castle hill. A small church stood in the very same place as early as the Middle Ages, but was torn down in 1550 due to Ottoman threat in the area. The church was rebuilt in 1661 in an early Baroque style. The church is consecrated to St. Nicholas, the patron of sailors. His statue is situated in the stone niche above the main entrance to the church. The church was originally Roman Catholic, but was later transformed into a Greek Catholic Church. In 1950, the Greek Catholic Church was heavily persecuted and this church was then transformed into an Orthodox Church.

MAP ▲ 13

7 JESUIT CHURCH

▼ The Jesuit Church

The number of German Protestants grew steadily in Bratislava during the 17th century. Eventually a Protestant church was built practically on the Main Square. As it was a Protestant church, it could not look like a sacral building. Notice that it does not have a tower and it is significantly larger than any other building on the Main Square. The church was built in 1638, but was taken away from the Protestants and given to the Jesuits in 1672. A column was placed in front of the church to symbolize the suppression of the Protestants.

MAP ▲ 14

8 BLUMENTAL

In 1888, the consecration of a new church east of the city-center was witnessed by some 30,000 people. Bratislava had a population of only around 70,000. This Romanesque Revival Cathedral has three naves and features an interesting interior.

MAP ● 1

PARKS

Parks are an essential part of any urban infrastructure and it's easy to spot that Bratislava is underpar in this area in comparison to other European cities.

▲ Grassalkovich palace as seen from the neatly maintained Grassalkovich garden

1 GRASSALKO-VICH GARDEN

This is also known as the Presidential Garden. The garden behind the Grassalkovich Palace is currently the only maintained French garden in Bratislava. The garden was constructed in 1760, the same time as the Palace, and was rebuilt to its original appearance in 1999. Although the Grassalkovich Palace is used for the residence of the President and is not open to the public, the garden is open all year long. The custom is that each time the President receives a foreign president, they plant an oak tree in this garden. The planted trees are located along the east fence. The park is open year-round, with shorter opening hours during the winter.

MAP ● 1 🕒 8:00 - 22:00

2 MEDIC GARDEN

Medic Garden was bought by Ccount Esterházy in the 19th century. He remodeled the garden to a Baroque garden with a wide variety of rare flowers. Unfortunately, no decorations were preserved and the garden slowly lost its charm. Today, it is the only green enclave in the densely built-up area around it. The name is derived from its close proximity to the Faculty of Medicine, Comenius University. Having a take-away lunch in the garden is a very good idea. The park is open year-round, with shorter opening hours in the winter.

MAP ● 2 🕒 8:00 - 22:00

3 SAD JANKA KRÁĽA

Literally meaning, "Orchard of Janko Kráľ", this is the largest park in Bratislava. It's located on the right bank of the Danube, just 10 minutes by foot from the city-center. The park was established in 1774-76; making it one of the oldest in Europe. The original Baroque classicism consisted of eight pathways; each lined with different trees (oak, maple, willow, etc.). It was redesigned to the

▼ Original gothic tower in sad Janka Kráľa

▼ Medic garden

present-day shape in 1839.

One interesting feature is the Gothic tower in the eastern part of the park. It was originally the tower of the Franciscan church (📄 71). An earthquake damaged the upper part of the tower in the 19th century. Afterward a replica was placed on top of the church and the original was moved into this park. Visiting the park is not regulated and although it is considered to be safe, we do not recommend visiting this park late at night.

MAP ◆2

▼ Sad Janka Kráľa

MEMORIALS

1 SLAVÍN MEMORIAL

Slavín is a memorial monument and a cemetery for fallen Soviet soldiers who died in Bratislava during World War II in April 1945. A total of 6845 soldiers are buried in 6 mass and 278 individual graves. On top of the 40 m obelisk is an 11-meter high sculpture of a soldier. The memorial and its location offer a nice view along with a quiet atmosphere. The memorial is freely accessible to the public.

MAP ⬤1

Slavín - Memorial for the 6845 soviet soldiers that died while freeing Bratislava ▼

▲ Tomb of Chatam Sófer; one of the leading European rabbis

2 CHATAM SOFER MEMORIAL

Moshe Schreiber was one of the leading European rabbis in the first half of the 19th century. He was a powerful opponent to the Reform Movement; which was ongoing in his time. He headed a yeshiva in Bratislava that was considered as one of the most prominent centers of traditional Jewish learning in Europe.

In 1943, a tunnel was constructed and destroyed a Jewish burial place. Only 22 graves surrounding the Chatam Sofer's tomb were spared. The site was redeveloped in 2002.

(📞 +421 2 54416949

FOUNTAINS

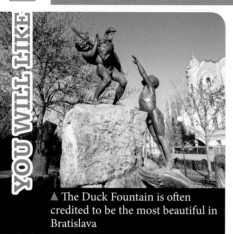

YOU WILL LIKE

▲ The Duck Fountain is often credited to be the most beautiful in Bratislava

Fountains were originally purely functional. They provided drinking water and water for bathing and washing to the residents of cities. Until the 19th century, fountains operated by gravity; which means they needed a source of water higher than the fountain. The water was delivered to the fountain by an aqueduct; which provided enough pressure for the water to flow or even jet out of the fountain. By the end of the 19th century, water in Bratislava was distributed to houses by plumbing so that most of the fountains were removed and those that were left serve as decorations to this day. The oldest fountain in Bratislava is Maximilian Fountain and it is located on the Main Square (📄 59). One of the most notable fountains in Bratislava is Ganymedes' Fountain in front of the opera house (📄 67).

1 DUCK FOUNTAIN

Slovak: Kačacia fontána. Although a little further from the city-center, this fountain is considered to be the most beautiful. It features elements from a folktale about a boy that a duck herder turned into stone. It was created in 1914 by sculptor Robert Kühmayer who is the maker of many statues in Slovakia; including a famous Barlolámač in Piešťany.

MAP ⭐2

2 BIRD'S FOUNTAIN

Slovak: Vtáčia fontána. Several copies of the same fountain were cast in 1900 and disbursed to multiple cities in Europe; including Bratislava. The original fountains were gradually removed and the last known fountain was on Račianske Square around the year 1950. In 2002, the city agreed with the owner of one of the fountains to make a replica; which was then placed on the corner of Ventúrska and Panská.

The fountain has a basin near the ground for cats and dogs and a small basin at the top for birds. The falling water from the top basin was used by the city's residents; while horses drank from the middle basin.

MAP ▲15

▼ Bird's Fountain: Our ancestors didn't like seeing the birds thirsty

3 PEACE FOUNTAIN

Slovak: Fontána mieru. Many fountains were built during the Communist Regime and the Peace Fountain on Hodžovo Square is one of them. The globe is 3 m in diameter and represents the world with negative reliefs of doves, a symbol of peace. The fountain was created and placed in front of the Grassalkovich Palace in 1982.

MAP ▲16

81 | Travel Guide

▲ Girl with her brother turned into a deer

5 GIRL WITH A DEER

Hviezdoslavovo Square is the home of possibly the cutest fountain in Bratislava. It gathered inspiration from a German tale about a girl and her brother who were turned into fawns by a curse. The fountain, made of red artificial stone, was started by Alojz Rigele, who died in 1938 and had therefore left the piece unfinished. Its construction was resumed and finished by Robert Kühmayer.

MAP ▲17

4 WOMAN WITH A JUG

Documents from 1561 state that this fountain was here as early as 1549. The fountain had a pillar with a lion on top. The lion remained there until it was weathered and worn and was then replaced with the current statue of a woman holding a jug. The statue was briefly moved to the Old Town Hall, but returned to the Františkánske Square in 1998. An interesting feature is that the lion which was previously on this fountain was moved a few times as well and it replica is now in front of the city market (MAP ▲M5), The original is preserved in the city's archive.

MAP ▲K6

▼ The Peace Fountain. One of many communist fountains in Bratislava

▼ Woman with a jug fountain

5 PEEING BOYS

The Maximilian fountain (📄 81), originally had a pillar segment depicting boys peeing. In the 18th century, society didn't appreciate the naked boys and had the segment replaced with more a appropriate one.

The original segment was used to create a new fountain which was placed in the courtyard of Ruttkay Palace on Uršulínska Street.

MAP ▲L6

BRIDGES

Before people could build bridges, the only way to cross a river was by using a boat or to simply wade through a ford. One of Danube's fords was approximately below the New Bridge and another was near the Devin Castle. Because of these two fords, Bratislava was the place where ancient trade routes crossed. A fee was required to cross the ford. As time progressed, people got tired of getting wet each time they crossed the Danube and started to build bridges. Since the Danube was not regulated, most of them didn't last longer than a year. Regulation in 1870-1890 made building a long-standing bridge possible. Bratislava's most notable bridge is the New Bridge (📄 69).

▲ Old Bridge - the oldest still-standing bridge in Bratislava.

1 OLD BRIDGE

Slovak: Starý most. The Old Bridge is the oldest bridge still standing in Bratislava. Its construction took 22 months and the bridge was finally inaugurated on December 30, 1890 by Emperor Franz Joseph; after whom the bridge was named. In first half of the 20th century, an electric tram line connecting Bratislava and Vienna ran across this bridge. The steel part of the bridge was completely destroyed during the World War II by retreating German forces. It was later rebuilt by German prisoners of war. Although this was meant to be only temporary, this was the only bridge in Bratislava until 1972 when the New Bridge was built. Due to

safety concerns, the Old Bridge was closed to car traffic in 2009 and its future is unclear.

 MAP ⬡ 1

▲ The Harbor Bridge carries over 100,000 cars each day

2 HARBOR BRIDGE

Slovak: Prístavný most. The Harbor Bridge is a two-tiered motorway-railroad truss bridge. It was built in 1977-1985 to relieve the city-center of the steadily increasing volumes of car traffic going to-and-from Petržalka. Today, it is a part of the Slovak highway system and connects the rest of Slovakia with Austria, Hungary and Czech republic. There are four lanes in the upper floor and a railroad with pedestrian pathways on the lower floor. The bridge was designed to handle 60,000 cars per day, but on average, over 100,000 cars cross this bridge each day.

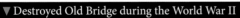

▼ Destroyed Old Bridge during the World War II

▲ Lafranconi Bridge

▲ Apollo Bridge

3 LAFRANCONI

Chronologically, Lafranconi was the forth bridge to be built in Bratislava and was built in the years 1985-1992. It is a part of highway D2 traversing north-to-south and provides access to Austria and Hungary. The bridge is 761 meters long and is 11 meters thick in some places. It was supposed to be named "Youth Bridge", but with the fall of Communism in Slovakia, it was renamed to Lafranconi Bridge after Italian engineer, Grazioso Enea Lanfranconi, who lived in Bratislava and worked on regulating the Danube River in the late 19th century.

4 APOLLO

The newest bridge in Bratislava was built in the years 2002-2005. The bridge was completely built on the left bank and was rotated across the river using a floating pontoon. The bridge received several international design awards. It is named after the refinery Apollo, which was bombarded by the US Air Forces during the WWII.

MAP ⬡ 2

LEFT OR RIGHT?

The standard use regarding the descriptive terms "left bank" and "right bank" are relative to an observer who is looking downstream.

Left

Right

▲ Apollo Bridge: The bridge was built on the left bank and rotated accross the river.

▼ New Bridge (📄 69): Considered the most notable Bridge in Bratislava

STATUES

▲ Čumil

one. It is said that he received free cake from local coffee shops. He was most probably mentally challenged, but was very popular amongst the residents of Bratislava who called him "Schöne Náci"; which in German means "nice Ignác" (although misspelled). He died of tuberculosis in 1967 with no living relatives to arrange the funeral.

MAP ▲ K7

1 ČUMIL

As a result of the city's initiative to attract more tourists to Bratislava, several bronze cast statues were installed in the city-center. Čumil, a man looking out of a manhole, is probably the most popular. The sculpture doesn't represent any real story. Čumil was damaged a few times by oncoming supply trucks which had overlooked the statue due to its low height and because of this, the city has placed a traffic sign nearby to ensure the statue's safety. The statue's designer is Viktor Hulík and it was installed in 1997.

MAP ▲ 18

2 SCHÖNE NÁCI

Contrary to Čumil, this statue represents a real person who was an icon in Bratislava. His real name was Ignác Lamár and he lived in the years 1897-1967. According to stories, his life was full of misfortune and existential problems. He became famous by walking in the city-center while wearing a velvet top hat and tails and greeting every-

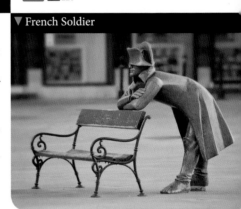

▼ French Soldier

3 FRENCH SOLDIER

A statue depicting a soldier of Napoleon's army is located in Main Square in front of the French Embassy. French soldiers were in Bratislava twice. The first time was in November 1905, when around 10,000 French soldiers peacefully conquered Bratislava. The army stayed for one and a half months, until a peace treaty between France and Austria was signed in Primate's Palace (📄 63). The peace treaty didn't last long and Napoleon's soldiers came again in 1909. Their visit was not peaceful this time. Napoleon's army bombarded Bratislava with 2,000-3,000 cannonballs per day but didn't manage to cross the Danube. Napoleon himself visited Bratislava after a new peace treaty was signed.

MAP ▲ K6

▼ Schöne Náci: Statue and a photo

4 HVIEZDOSLAV

One of the biggest statues in the city-center is the Hviezdoslav statue located on Hviezdoslav Square. The statue was unveiled in front of over 15,000 people in 1937. Hviezdoslav was a renowned Slovak poet and dramatist who lived in the years 1849-1921.

▲ Hviezdoslav statue

MAP ▲ L8

5 ŠTEFÁNIK AND CZECH LION

Two statues are located on a square in the Eurovea Galleria shopping center. Štefánik was a notable Slovak politician and diplomat who contributed decisively to the cause of Czechoslovak sovereignty. The lion is holding a Czechoslovak (now Czech) coat of arms. There is an interesting history behind these two statues. They were unveiled together in 1938 on Ľudovít Štúr Square. A short year later, German forces came to Bratislava and Hitler himself give the order to remove the Lion statue. It is believed he said: "The cat must go".

▼ Statue of Štefánik with a lion

The lion was moved to a warehouse where it stayed until 1988 when it was placed in front of the National Museum. While Hitler didn't mind the Štefánik statue, Communist officials did. The statue was destroyed in 1954. In 2009, the two statues were reunited, although Štefánik's only as a replica.

MAP ⭐ 3

MILAN RASTISLAV ŠTEFÁNIK

Born in 1880 as one of 13 children, he was a strong Slovak patriot from a very young age. He attended philosophy lectures taught by Tomáš Garrigue Masaryk, who later became the first president of Czechoslovakia.

He moved to France, where he became interested in astronomy, meteorology, and eventually got a job which allowed him to travel around the world and carry out various political tasks.

After the outbreak of World War I, Štefánik believed that it was the right moment to push for the independence of Czechoslovakia from Austria-Hungary. The independence was declared on October 28, 1918, but disputes around the position of Slovakia within Czechoslovakia arose soon after.

REMAINS OF COMMUNISM

Slovakia was under the Communist Regime during the years 1948-1989. Some of the buildings built in these years are attractive, but most are not appealing at all. Architecture of this era is characterized by the vast use of concrete, small windows, and a very functionalist approach. The Communist Regime, didn't invest in the city-center and so nearly all of the facades needed to be re-made after 1989.

▲▼ Paneláks in Petržalka

2 PETRŽALKA

Petržalka is a borough of Bratislava with the highest concentration of paneláks in Central Europe. The construction of the panel houses started in 1977 and now around 130,000 people live in them.

This borough was often connected with a high crime rate and drug dealing. This problem seems to have disappeared, with exception of some areas, and now Petržalka doesn't stand out in terms of crime statistics. It is the most densely-populated residential district in Central Europe.

3 TV TOWER

This massive television broadcasting tower was built in 1975. It is 194 meters high and stands on a 433-meter high hill; which guarantees proper signal propagation. It is also the first visible structure when arriving to Bratislava. The tower broadcasts several radio stations and two government-owned TV stations.

▲ TV tower

1 PANELÁK

A panelák is a type of government-built housing. To solve housing shortages, Communist leaders employed a strategy to build many uniform prefabricated buildings over the whole country. In total, 1.17 million flats were built. They house 3.5 million people or about one third of Czechs and Slovaks today. Many people criticize them for their low design quality, mind-numbing appearance and second-rate construction materials. As a recent trend, many paneláks are being insulated and painted. This, in addition to saving on the cost of heating, makes them somewhat nicer.

4 SLOVAK RADIO

This very interesting building was the first to use steel construction in Bratislava. The design was created in 1967, but the building was finished in 1983. The design resembles a pyramid turned upside down, which although amusing, proved to be impractical.

▲ Slovak Radio: Inverted pyramid

▼ Hotel Kyjev

▼ Prior: department store around 1985.

For example, the rooms inside are dark because the sunlight is blocked by the upper floors. The building houses several recording studios and a concert hall.

MAP ●3

5 PRIOR AND HOTEL KYJEV

Believe it or not, this complex, consisting of a department store and a hotel, was regarded to have state-of-the-art architecture when it was built. The design for the two buildings was developed in 1960. In 1968, over 40,000 people came at 6:00 a.m. to see the opening of the largest department store in Czechoslovakia; topping even department stores in Prague. The hotel was opened in 1973.

Today, the department store is operated by Tesco and Hotel Kyjev was scheduled for demolition in 2007, but it was postponed by the city indefinitely.

MAP ★4

6 SLOVAK NATIONAL GALLERY

The Slovak National Gallery was originally in Martin, a city in central Slovakia. It was later moved to Bratislava to a building on the Danube's riverside called "Water Barracks". This building soon proved to be too small to house all of the Gallery's items. The south wing was demolished and a 70 meter long extension was built in 1977. This extension is considered controversial and many think it doesn't fit into Bratislava's riverside aesthetic.

MAP ▲19

▼ Extension of the Slovak National Gallery

WHAT TO DO

MUSEUMS

We recommend you visit some of Bratislava's museums to explore the rich history and culture of this area.

MUSEUM OF HISTORY

Slovak: Historické múzeum. The Museum of History displays almost 250,000 objects from a broad-range of fields including: national history, arts, sculpting, painting, culture, numismatics, ethnography, warfare and economy. Several collections of this museum are the largest in Slovakia (numismatics, historical and traditional textile, glass and ceramics, militaria, crafts, historical press, sacral and folk plastic and fine arts). The Museum of History is located in the Bratislava Castle and is open daily; except Mondays.

MAP ▲**1** 🕐 10:00 - 18:00
📞 +421 2 20483111 🔖 snm.sk 💶 € 2.50

The Museum of City History ▼

MUSEUM OF CITY HISTORY

Slovak: Múzeum dejín mesta. This museum features a vast collection of items related to the history of Bratislava. The collection is very wide in scope and ranges from ancient-to-modern, from art-to-economy and covers all aspects of how Bratislava evolved to its present-day appearance. In addition, you can visit a historical jail and a town hall tower with a nice view. The Museum of City History is located in the Old Town Hall and is open daily except Mondays.

MAP ▲**4** 🕐 11:00 - 17:00
📞 +421 2 59100812 🔖 bratislava.sk 💶 € 5

▲ Cannon in front of the Museum of Arms

MUSEUM OF ARMS

The museum has tons of weapons on display. These include: giant swords, muskets, heavy armor and shields. The top floor provides access to an observation deck. The museum is located at Michael's Gate and is open daily; except Mondays. The entrance is a small wooden door just next to the gate.

MAP ▲**6** 🕐 11:00 - 17:00
📞 +421 2 54433044 💶 € 4.30

MUSEUM OF JEWISH CULTURE

Slovak: Múzeum židovskej kultúry. The permanent exhibition is housed in the original late-Renaissance Zsigray Mansion. The museum explains the everyday life of the Jewish population living in the territory of Slovakia from as early as the times of the Great Moravian Empire. The most valuable items on display are two jugs from the years 1734 and 1776. Part of the museum is dedicated to the memory of the Holocaust. The museum is open daily; except Saturdays.

MAP ▲**H6** 🕐 11:00 - 17:00
📞 +421 2 20490109 🔖 snm.sk 💶 € 7

ARCHEOLOGICAL MUSEUM

Slovak: Archeologické múzeum. The exhibition presents over 150,000 objects; most of which are archaeological findings spanning from the Early Stone Age to the Late Middle Ages. The museum also houses a Lapidarium (a collection of stone artifacts), reconstructions and video exhibits. The Archeological museum is located in the Renaissance-style building of the Kamper Mansion; which dates from the 16th century and is open daily; except Tuesdays.

MAP ▲D9 🕐 10:00 - 17:00
📞 +421 2 59207275 📶 snm.sk € € 3

Cars in the Transport Museum ▼

TRANSPORT MUSEUM

Slovak: Múzeum dopravy. The museum is situated in a beautiful setting of historical buildings of the first railway station from the 19th century and features collections of historical road vehicles, bicycles, car prototypes and military vehicles. The oldest exhibit is a Praga car from 1911. You will also find steam, diesel and electric locomotives of the 19th and 20th centuries along with railroad-related items, like uniforms or even a steam crane. The museum is located near the Main Train Station and is open daily; except Mondays.

MAP ●I1 🕐 10:00 - 17:00
📞 +421 2 52444163
📶 muzeumdopravy.com € € 3.30

▲ Skeleton found at Gerulata

GERULATA

Gerulata was a Roman military camp that was built in the 2nd century as a part of the Limes Romanus system. Limes Romanus was a border defense system of the Roman Empire which stretched over 5,000 km from the Atlantic coast of northern Britain, through Europe to the Black Sea, and from there to the Red Sea and then across North Africa to the Atlantic coast. Gerulata was abandoned in the 4th century, when Roman legions withdrew from the region.

The museum consists of several outdoor objects which were partially reconstructed so that the foundations of the buildings can be visible. The most preserved object is a quadrilateral building 30 meters long and 30 meters wide with 2.4 meter thick walls. The museum is located 10 km south of the city-center and is open in the summer season daily; except Mondays.

📅 Apr - Oct 🕐 10:00 - 17:00 📞 +421 2 62859332 € € 2.30

NATURAL HISTORY MUSEUM

Slovak: Prírodovedné múzeum. The museum features nearly 4 million items; which makes it one of the most significant natural history museums in Europe. The museum exhibits include: plants, animals, fossils, minerals, rocks, meteorites, and human cultural artifacts. The museum is located on the riverfront close to city-center and is open daily; except Mondays.

MAP ★A9 🕐 10:00 - 17:00
📞 +421 2 59349122 📶 snm.sk € € 3.50

VISUAL ARTS

SLOVAK NATIONAL GALLERY

Slovak: Slovenská národná galéria. The largest art exposition in Slovakia is located on the waterfront in two adjacent buildings; the Esterházy Palace and the Water Barracks. The gallery showcases fine Slovak Gothic, Garoque and twentieth-century art in addition to some old European art pieces. It's open daily; except Mondays.

MAP ▲ **19** 🕐 10:00 - 18:00 📞 +421 2 59226270 🖋 sng.sk 💶 € 3.50

▲ Buildings of Slovak National Gallery located on the waterfront

BRATISLAVA CITY GALLERY

Slovak: Galéria mesta Bratislava. It's the second largest Slovak gallery and is located in two historical buildings; the Mirbach Palace and the Pálffy Palace. The gallery currently contains approximately 35,000 works of art; which were collected from as early as the 19th century. The gallery is open to the public daily; except Mondays.

MAP ▲ **K5** 🕐 11:00 - 18:00 📞 +421 2 54431556 🖋 gmb.sk 💶 € 3.50

DANUBIANA

This modern art museum is not located in the city-center, but approximately 15 km south of Bratislava in Čunovo. The location is very interesting since the building is built on the tip of a peninsula in the middle of the Danube River. If you find modern art interesting and have a means of transportation, consider visiting this unique art museum. The location is accessible by car, bus or by a designated bicycle route (📋 103).

🕐 10:00 - 18:00 📞 +421 2 62528501 🖋 danubiana.eu 💶 € 4

PERFORMING ARTS

Bratislava's well-established performing arts are very popular amongst international visitors due to the good quality and very reasonable price. The Slovak National Theater offers a wide-selection of opera, ballet and theatrical performances. Since 2007, most of the plays have been moved to a new building located next to the Danube River. It's a little further from the city-center, but some performances are still being held in the historical building. These are a bit more expensive, but the atmosphere of an evening event in a classy venue is worth it.

OPERA

For more than 90 years, Bratislava has had two venues where opera is performed. The first is the beautiful and historical Slovak National Theater located in the city-center (📄 67) and the new building of the Slovak National Theater located adjacent to the Eurovea shopping center (**MAP** ⭐3). Opera performances have subtitles in Slovak or German, but booklets with an English transcript can be purchased on location. The season starts in September and ends in June with performances more or less daily; except on Sundays. Expect to pay € 25.00 for the best seat and € 8.00 for a balcony seat.

HOW TO BUY TICKETS

Tickets can be purchased in advance at box offices or online at: www.ticketmaster.sk. The box offices are located in both the new and historical buildings of the Slovak National Theater and are open Monday-through-Friday.

MAP ▲7 🕐 8:00 - 19:00 📞 +421 2 20472298, +421 2 20494290 🔗 snd.sk

▼ The new building of the Slovak National Theater(**MAP** ⭐6)

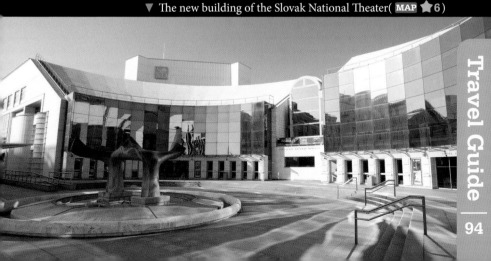

MUSIC

SLOVAK PHILHARMONIC ORCHESTRA

Bratislava is the home of the world-famous Slovak Philharmonic Orchestra. So, if you like classical music, we highly recommend you attend one of the concerts which are held in the beautiful 18th century Baroque building called Reduta. The Slovak Philharmonic Orchestra was founded in 1949 and produced many critically acclaimed recordings of European classical music.

Tickets can be purchased during work days or one hour before each concert at the historical Slovak National Theater building located across the Reduta on Hviezdoslavovo námestie.

MAP ▲L9 (C) +421 2 20475233 📞 filharmonia.sk € € 4 - € 20

▲ Interior of the Reduta, venue of Slovak Philharmonic Orchestra concerts

FOLK MUSIC

Slovakia is an enormous reservoir for folk music. Much of it originated from sacred music and creativity to entertain the workers during manual agricultural labor. In 1526, Bratislava became a coronation city and this was to greatly influence the development of formal music in the city.

Slovakia's notable folk instruments include the fujara, a 150 to 170 cm long shepherd's fipple flute. The instrument has three tone-holes, but when overblown it can play the whole didactic scale.

CLASSICAL MUSIC

In the 18th century, the Viennese musical influence quickly spread to Bratislava. Many of the city's palaces and their nobility hosted musical bodies regularly and some even had

▲ This memorial tablet at Pálffy Palace is an error. He performed in a different building, also called Pálffy Palace.

Memorial tablet at the Leopold de Pauli Palace commemorating Liszt's concert ▼

their own music ensembles to keep them entertained. In the second half of the 18th century, many of the musical personalities visited Bratislava. Wolfgang Amadeus Mozart visited in 1762 and performed in the Pálffy Palace (**MAP** ▲**F5**) when he was only six-years old. Unfortunately, this was the only visit by Mozart. Joseph Haydn was born very close-by in Rohrau, an Austrian city approximately 25 km to the west. He premiered his works regularly in the Grassalkovich Palace (**MAP** ▲**K1**); which was the center of musical culture at the time. Ludwig van Beethoven visited Bratislava in 1796 for nine days while touring Europe.

FRANZ LISZT

Franz Liszt, a talented nine-year old boy, came to Bratislava to give a concert in 1820. His performance was so good that it attracted some wealthy sponsors to finance his musical education. Later he received piano lessons from Carl Czerny, who, in his own youth, had been a student of Beethoven and Hummel. He also received lessons in composition from Antonio Salieri, who was at that time the music director of the Viennese court. This boy grew up to be regarded as one of the Hungary's greatest composers.

BÉLA BARTÓK

Bratislava continued to be interested in music in the 20th century. Béla Bartók, a renowned composer and pianist, moved to Bratislava with his mother after his father died. He was eight-years old at that time. During his school days, he spent his time collecting Hungarian and Slovak folk songs; some of which he later adapted into his own pieces. After finishing high school, he once again moved to Budapest and later, in 1940, immigrated to New York, where he lived the rest of his life.

COMMUNIST REGIME

In the second half of the 20th century, during the Communist Regime, musical culture played an important role in Communist Propaganda. The government used radio jammers against Western broadcasts and all of the songs to be made available to public had to be approved by the Communist party. In spite of all of its effort, music produced in Czechoslovakia was of quite good quality and was undeniably under the influence of Western music that had been smuggled across borders in various forms.

▼ Béla Bartók in 1927

CITY TOURS

Tourism is still developing in Bratislava. Tour operators tend to come and go and although many offer daily city tours, it is surprisingly hard to find a guided-tour if you don't happen to be in a group.

OLDTIMER®

This red guided-tour bus will take you through the city-center on a 30 minute round-trip tour. It begins at the Main Square. No reservation is required. Narrated commentary is provided in a wide-range of languages.

📅 Apr - Oct 📞 +421 903 302817 🖂 tour4u.sk

RIVER CRUISES

The Danube River is certainly one of Bratislava's highlights and if you have already strolled along it or crossed it by bridge, it is time to travel via the river itself.

TWIN CITY LINER®

This high-speed catamaran makes up to 5 daily round-trips between Bratislava and Vienna. The journey takes 90 minutes (75 minutes downstream) and provides beautiful views along the way. The ship offers both panoramic windows and an open air deck. Catering is provided. Dogs and bicycles are allowed. This is the fastest way to get from one city-center to another. The first departure from Bratislava is at 10:30 and the last departure from Vienna is at 18:00 (select days only). Tickets can be purchased at a ticket stand at the waterfront.

MAP ▲20 📅 Apr - Oct 📞 +43 1 58880

🖂 twincityliner.com 💶 € 19 - € 33 (one way)

SIGHTSEEING CRUISE

A 45 minute sightseeing cruise, which passes under the five bridges spanning the Danube River, provides panoramic views of Bratislava. The sightseeing boat features a closed lower-deck and an open air upper-deck. No reservation is required.

MAP ▲21 📅 Apr - Sep 📞 +421 2 52932226 🖂 lod.sk 💶 € 5

NIGHT LIFE

Bratislava's club scene is a bit shy. Not many clubs offer large enough dance floors and most of them permit smoking. If the club looks good, expect the pricing to be set accordingly. The clubs generally open around 9 p.m. and close early in the morning. Some clubs are open daily, but the biggest club nights are, of course, Friday and Saturday. Expect to pay around € 2.00 for a beer.

Eight colleges are located in Bratislava with around 60,000 students, so the city, especially around the campuses is very "alive" during school semesters.

BRATISLAVA FOR KIDS

ŽELEZNÁ STUDIENKA

This is a nice forested park with recently-built play-grounds, basketball and volleyball courts, outdoor grills, refreshment kiosks and public restrooms. This is probably the most suitable children's play environment in Bratislava at the moment.

To get there, take trolleybus #212 from Mierovo námestie and ride all the way to the terminal stop.

(C) +421 910 123451

BIBIANA

Founded in 1987, this self-proclaimed international house of art is an interesting cultural institution. Basically it is an art museum for children which offers various exhibits, workshops and houses a library. Some children find this interesting, while some do not.

MAP ▲I9 🕙 10:00 - 18:00 (C) +421 2 54434986 📎 bibiana.sk € € 0.70 - € 1.20

In addition to these suggestions, you might consider visiting the Zoo (📄 103), the botanical garden(📄 104), or a water park (📄 106).

SHOPPING

Shopping in Bratislava is comfortable due to many recently built shopping malls. Most of the shops in the malls are open daily from 9:00 to 21:00 and most of them will accept all major payment cards. All of the major shopping malls include a selection of fast food and casual dining restaurants as well as cafes.

EUROVEA GALLERIA

The newest shopping mall is located downstream on Danube's riverside. The three-floor shopping mall is connected to the city-center by a nice pedestrian walkway. The trip by foot takes only 15 minutes. Eurovea Galleria features: a modern design, more than 180 stores, 60,000 m2 of retail space, an 8-screen multiplex and 1,729 parking spaces. Parking is generally paid, but promotions may apply(free on weekends, evenings, 3 hrs, etc.). The food court offers a selection of fast food restaurants (McDonald's, Burger King) and a variety of ethnic restaurants (Mexican, Italian, Slovak, etc.). If the weather allows, we recommend getting a meal to go and eating it riverside. Eurovea's unique element is the glass dome roof made of 2,300 triangles.

MAP ⭐ 3 (☎) +421 2 20915050
📞 eurovea.com

▲▼ Eurovea shopping mall

AUPARK

The shopping mall is located on the south bank of the Danube River and is in walking-distance from the city-center (20 min). To get there, just cross the New Bridge (📖 69) and continue through a large park (Sad Janka Krála, 📖 79) until you arrive at a distinguishable shopping mall. Aupark houses 240 shops on a total area of 58,000 m2. There is also: a 12-screen multiplex with digital projection, 2,300 free parking spaces, a health club, hair salons, a nail studio and a playground. If you don't like walking, there are multiple bus connections to-and-from the city-center.

MAP ◆ 3 (☎) +421 2 68266111
📞 aupark.sk

▼ Aupark shopping mall

MY BRATISLAVA

This department store is operated by Tesco directly in the city-center on Kamenné námestie. You will find a wide selection of: clothing brands, health products, home electronics, office supplies, home accessories and a Tesco grocery store situated on 12,000 m2 of retail space. If you need batteries for a camera or a decent grocery store, this is the place.

MAP ⭐5 (C) +421 2 59218111 🍃 itesco.sk

AVION

The largest shopping mall in Bratislava is located on highway D1, just 8 km east of city-center. You will find 155 stores and 11 restaurants on 84,000 m2 of retail space. This includes IKEA and a large hypermarket. Parking is provided by 3,000 free parking spaces. Hornbach, a home improvement chain store, is nearby. This shopping mall is accessible by bus #61 from the Main Train Station.

(C) +421 2 48226800 🍃 avion.sk

FOLK CRAFTS

Local crafts include various hand painted ceramics, hand weaved textiles and woodwork. Corn husk dolls make for a nice handmade souvenir, try to buy one with packaging to prevent the damage whilst transporting it home.

You can easily recognize a handmade item by a sticker saying so and higher price.

▼ The detail on Slovak ceramics is amazing   ▲ Corn husk doll

LEISURE

CYCLING

Cycling is very popular in Bratislava, but mostly as a recreational sport. Use of bicycle as a way of transportation is very limited due to the poor cycling infrastructure in the city.

DANUBE BIKE TRAIL

Bratislava has one of the best bicycle trails in Europe; the Danube Bike Trail. This mostly designated bicycle

▲ The designated cycling routes are car-free and ideal for family trips

trail runs along the Danube river from its source in Germany all the way to its mouth in the Black Sea for a total of 2,875 km in length. If you are staying in Bratislava for a longer period of time, we highly recommend you get a bicycle and explore this trail a bit.

BRATISLAVA - RUSOVCE

▼ Archeological site in Rusovce

This is the most popular bicycle trail for locals and it gets very crowded on weekends. It is flat, has a good surface and overall provides a very easy trip. Refreshments are available along the trail. Rusovce is around 15 km southeast along the Danube Bike Trail. The trip itself is nice and you will find a smaller lake at the end. In the Rusovce district, you will find ruins of Gerulata, a Roman military camp built in the 2nd century as a part of the Limes Romanus system.

BRATISLAVA - ČUNOVO

The bicycle ride 20 km downstream along the Danube will get you to Čunovo where you will find a smaller dam, a water sports center (📄 106) and a modern art museum named Danubiana (📄 93). The trail is very flat and is considered to be easy, but since the trail leads along the Danube it might get windy during the day.

BRATISLAVA ZOO

🕐 9:00 - 18:00 📞 +421 2 60102111 🔗 zoobratislava.sk 💶 € 4.50

The Bratislava Zoo extends over 96 hectares and provides a home for 656 animals comprising 157 species. The zoo was built in 1960. It underwent a major reduction from 1981-1985, when a highway that was been being built nearby reduced the land area to just one-third. The second reduction occurred in 2003 when a highway tunnel was built. This forced the relocation of the entrance gate. The zoo attracts 300,000 visitors annually. Amongst others, the Bratislava Zoo features: white lions, Sri Lankan leopards, rhinoceroses, kanga-

▼ The dinopark might be quite scary for younger children

roos and many other animal exhibits.

DINOPARK

In 2004, the zoo added a small dinosaur-themed park with 22 full-scale dinosaur replicas. The replicas are equipped with a sound system to provide a genuine Mesozoic Era environment. Along with replicas, the park features a theater which shows an educational 3D movie. Access to the park, along with the 3D movie, is open to all zoo visitors at no additional cost.

WOLLEMI PINE

Dating back to the days of the dinosaurs, the 200-million year old Wollemi pine tree is one of the oldest plants on Earth and is one of the rarest. Less than 100 adult trees are known to exist in the wild; thus placing the Wollemi pine tree at the heart of one of the world's most extensive conservation campaigns. Since 2006, one of these trees is on display in the Dinopark section of the zoo.

GETTING THERE

The zoo is accessible by buses #30, #31, #32 - departing from the Main Train Station and also from: #37, #39, #92. You need to get off at the "zastávka ZOO" bus stop. The zoo is open year round, but shorter opening hour apply in the winter.

BOTANICAL GARDEN

📅 Apr - Oct 🕙 9:00 - 18:00 📞 +421 2 65421311 € € 3.00

For quiet and peaceful strolls visit the Botanical garden of Comenius University. Across 50,000 m² , the Botanical garden features six indoor collections and more than fifteen outdoor expositions. Amongst many more, you will find rose garden with over 120 rose species, greenhouses filled with exotic trees, palm trees.

▼ Insider tip: great dating spot

ROSE GARDEN

The Botanical Garden offers a romantic setting for enjoying time together while visiting Bratislava. The gardens bloom with roses each year and make a picturesque setting. Stroll through the romantic setting while enjoying the relaxing aroma and pleasing color of various rose blossoms.

GETTING THERE

The botanical garden is accessible by buses #28, #29 and #32, and by trams #1, #4, #5 and #9. The connections run through the "Kapucínska" tram stop (MAP ▲I5), the "Nový most" bus stop (MAP ▲I10) and the "Main Train Station" bus stop (MAP ●7). Exit at the "Botanická záhrada" stop. The botanical garden will be to your left when arriving from the city-center.

HIKING

While Bratislava is not exactly a mountain city, there are some lighter hiking opportunities nearby. If you are looking for world-class hiking, catch a 4-hour train ride to High Tatras.

DEVÍNSKA KOBYLA

This is easily the best hike in Bratislava. The one-way, 6 km long trail starts at Devínska Nová Ves and ends at Devín Castle and offers plenty of views along the way. Start by taking bus #93 from the 'Zochová' bus stop (**MAP** ▲H4), change to bus #21 at the 'Predstaničné nám.' bus stop. Then, exit at the 'Hradištná' stop. From there, just follow the green trail signs southeast. The trail soon passes the final houses and dips into a light forest where

you will find an educational project called Dendropark, which explains about historical trees in this area. If you are done educating yourself, continue on the green trail. You should reach Devínska Kobyla (514 m) after about 3 kilometers. Enjoy the view and start heading toward Devín Castle on the trail marked with red signs. If it's not too late, be sure to check out the castle (📄 127) as well. You can either backtrack to Devínska Nová Ves or take bus #29 back to the city center.

KAMZÍK CABLE CAR

This very popular Sunday afternoon hike is perfect for families and has a cable car ride as a bonus. This hike leads through forest on a well-surfaced paved road with a slight

gradient. It ends at Kamzik where the TV tower is located. While you can do this hike one-way with public transportation available at both ends, you can be creative and explore the area a little bit more using well-marked trails. Start by taking trolleybus #212 at the 'Hodžovo nám.' bus stop (**MAP** ▲16) and exit at the terminal stop. From there, continue slightly uphill, directly north. You will find a recreational area with playgrounds, public grills, two lakes and sporting equipment. Continue on the paved road 3 km and you will find a cable car station to your right. This cable car will take you to Kamzík (420 m) on a nearly 1 km long ride. From Kamzík, take the green flagged trail to Koliba where trolleybus #203 will take you back to the city-center or take the red flagged trail which leads back to where you started.

The cable car runs more or less daily in summer and from Thursday-to-Sunday during the off-season.

Travel Guide

📞 +421 2 44259188 💶 € 3 (one way)

WATER FUN

AQUAPARK SENEC

Aquapark Senec is easily accessible from the highway and is located 25 km east of Bratislava. This water park and wellness center is open year round. In the winter this facility offers two indoor pools with water temperatures between 32-36 °C, two outdoor pools, one water slide and a sauna and wellness center. The sauna and wellness center have many features; which amongst others, include: a Finnish dry sauna, a steam sauna, a salt sauna, a Turkish sauna, an outdoor dry sauna and 3 massage pools. Classic, Thai and sothys massages are offered.

May-through-August is considered the summer season and this is when an adjacent complex of pools and waterslides open. This makes Aquapark Senec perfect for both family fun and relaxing.

🕓 10:00 - 22:00 📞 +421 2 45648021 🌐 aquathermal.sk € € 12 (3hrs) - € 22 (full day)

WATER SPORTS CENTER ČUNOVO

Located 20 km downstream on the south bank of the Danube, this facility offers a wide range of watersports including: rafting, kayaking, wakeboarding and Jet Ski rental. The center has two whitewater channels. The longer is 460 meters long and has a stream flow of 12 m3/sec If you happen to have a captain's license, there is also a boat rental. It is accessible by car or by a designated cycling route along Danube's River bank (📄 103).

🕓 8:00 - 20:00 📅 Apr - Sep 📞 +421 905 313429 🌐 divokavoda.sk € € 20 and up

KAYAK AND CANOE RENTAL

Renting a boat and paddling around in one of Danube's branches is a lot of fun. There is no current, so it's ok if you are a complete beginner. Paddler is located approximately 2 km upstream from the city-center. They have all of the required equipment and if necessary, they will also provide an instructor.

📅 Year-round 📞 +421 2 20602020 🌐 paddler.sk € € 3 and up

WELLNESS

GOLEM HEALTH CLUB

Upscale health club chain with four locations in Bratislava in major shopping malls(Aupark, Eurovea, Avion). Fitness center with various indoor sports available including squash, aerobic, indoor cycling, pilates.

📄 99 🕓 6:00 - 22:00 📞 +421 0917 508649 🌐 golemclub.sk € € 3.50 and up

WHERE TO STAY

General information
Star ratings | Costs | Hotel chains

GENERAL INFORMATION

Based on where you are from or where have you traveled before, finding an appropriate accommodation in Bratislava can be a bit harder than elsewhere.

Remember that everything privately owned tends to be quite new and that tourism is still developing. Many hotels have inexperienced management and the hotel is just waiting to go under.

DO YOUR HOMEWORK

Try to check the hotel's reviews before you book it. If you don't do this, you are risking being ripped-off or worse. Many hotels in Bratislava operate on the assumption that the guest will stay there only once, so what's the point in trying.

STAR RATINGS

Nearly every hotel has stars prominently displayed at the front facade next to its name. What do these stars mean?

▲ Some hotels serve generous breakfast

Well, just about anything. The star ratings are provided by the government and are based on hotel amenities only. So basically, although a hotel might have a hair dryer in each bathroom, the linens can still smell and staff can be awfully rude.

COSTS

Don't expect accommodation to be cheaper than elsewhere in Europe. Having fewer tourists apparently doesn't guarantee lower prices. Instead, there are fewer hotels and all with the same prices.

A good estimate is € 15 for a hostel and € 50 and up for a hotel. The prices usually don't include the city tax; which is € 1.65 per person per night.

Another interesting habit is that often the same room costs more if occupied by two people instead of just one.

PAYING

At higher-class hotels you pay as you check-out. At guesthouses, hostels and budget hotels expect to pay for all nights upfront. If you are unsure how many nights you will spend, ask if you could pay for each night separately in the morning.

HOTEL CHAINS

Not many hotels in Bratislava operate under a chain brand. If you prefer this option prepare yourself to pay premium.

Some of the hotel brands that operate in Bratislava include: Best Western, Holiday Inn, Park Inn, Radisson, Sheraton, Kempinski and Hilton.

SHOULD I BOOK?

Tourism in Bratislava has recently been quite unpredictable. If you plan to stay here during July-August, definitely book your accommodation in advance; especially if your budget is limited. If you travel during off-season months or if you don't mind spending € 150 or more, then don't bother with booking, they will have a room for you.

▲ Good personnel is a sign of good hotel management

BED BUGS

Bed bugs are not common in Slovakia. Although, if the accommodation you've chosen doesn't seem to be perfectly clean, try to request to see the room and check for bugs under the mattress before paying.

NEGOTIATING

Negotiating is not common in Slovakia and the receptionists working the front office often don't like it. While you can try to get a lower price, it might anger the receptionist.

BREAKFAST

The majority of hotels offer breakfast, which is either included in the room price or for a surcharge. Many times this breakfast is more generous than in Western Europe or in the United States. This is especially true in private guesthouses where you might get an authentic Slovak home-cooked breakfast.

PRICES

The lowest reasonable price you could expect is € 15 per person per night. A good hotel in the city-center should be around € 70 and for a luxury hotel, expect to pay over € 200 per night.

AIR CONDITIONING

The majority of hotels don't have air conditioning since it's not common in Slovakia. If you are used to sleeping in an air-conditioned room, ask the clerk.

PARKING

If you plan on arriving by car, always ask if the hotel provides parking. The further the hotel is from the city-center the more problem-free the parking will be. Don't forget that the city-center is a car-free area.

SMOKING

Smoking in a non-smoking room could result in a fine and if you pay by your credit card, the fine can be charged after you check out. If you plan to smoke in your room, always ask beforehand.

EATING AND DRINKING

SLOVAK CUISINE

The origins of Slovak cuisine can be traced back to times when most people lived in small villages without the possibility to import or trade food. They cooked from the ingredients they had grown or made themselves or traded for at local village markets.

The cuisine differs geographically between Slovakia's northern part and southern part dramatically.

▲ Slovak "farmers" of northern Slovakia

NORTHERN CUISINE

Northern Slovakia is very mountainous. Winters are rough and last at least three months. The people had to plan for these months and stock up on food supplies, but because there were no modern means of preservation, the cuisine was very dependent on food that would not spoil. These ingredients included potatoes, wheat, sauerkraut, onion and various milk products.

The Northern cuisine is considered as Slovak, while cuisine of Southern Slovakia is very similar to Hungarian cuisine, since it is populated by people of Hungarian descendant.

SOUTHERN CUISINE

The Southern plains provided very hot summers and mild winters. Instead of storing potatoes, people here grew all kinds of fruit and vegetables and made jams and other products from it.

MEAT

Pork became the staple of local cuisine after the era of the Turkish invasion. Since Muslims are forbidden to eat pork, they left the pigs to natives. The meat was processed to make it last through the winter. It was either smoked or made into sausage. The Southern part is notable for cooking duck, goose and turkey.

BREAD

Traditional Slovak bread is sour and baked in large loafs. It was probably the most basic food and was consumed either with animal fat, butter or as a side dish to the majority of main dishes.

Several loaves were baked once per week. One was used that day and the others were wrapped in cloths to make them last for the rest of the week.

Variations are made by adding potatoes, cumin, buttermilk or sunflower seeds to the bread.

▲ Slovak bread: large, dark and heavy.

SALAŠ

Salaš is a shed with a barn or pens for sheep husbandry. The foreman is called "Bača". The sole purpose of Salaš is to collect wool and milk from sheep. Sheep are rarely used for meat.

Today, only a handful of salašes remain. Most of them serve as museums or for Agritourism. Some still sell their fresh dairy products.

BRYNDZA

Bryndza is a traditional Slovak soft cheese made of sheep's milk. Production of Bryndza in Slovakia started in the 15th century by Vlachs who were Romanian people that had migrated to present-day Slovakia. So while it's regarded as a typical Slovak product, it has Romanian roots.

Although this cheese can be bought pre-packaged, you can be more authentic and ask for it at the fresh cheese counter.

PARENICA

In addition to Bryndza, Slovakia offers a wide-range of smoked and non-smoked cheese in various forms.

If you find yourself in a supermarket, try to find "Parenica". It is a rolled smoked cheese that you can eat while you unroll it into thin strings. It's tasty and fun to eat.

▲▼ Bryndza is made from only the cutest sheep's milk. How could you not like it, right?

HOW TO DINE

EATING HABITS

Traditionally, lunch is the day's main meal. It is eaten around noon. It consists of soup and a main meal. Breakfast is often very light and consists of a sandwich, yogurt or a piece of fruit. Cooking for breakfast is not common. Dinner consists traditionally of one cooked meal without soup.

Most restaurants offer a daily special during lunch hours. These meals are pre-cooked in large quantities so they are generally of better quality than quickly prepared À la carte items.

SEATING

In most restaurants you can seat yourself wherever you would like, don't wait at the door to be seated. After you are seated, the waiter will come and set up the table.

PAYING

After you are done with your meal the waiter will bring you a check. Most often, every waiter has his own wallet and you can pay him right when he brings the bill. He will also give you change right away.

If you wish to tip, say the amount you want to pay when handing over the money. If you are paying with a payment card, say the amount when handing the card or leave a tip in cash.

THANK YOU

Saying "thank you" when paying means that you don't wish to receive change back. Beware of this because you can cause an awkward situation.

For example, if your total is € 2.30 and you hand over € 10 bill and say "thank you", the waiter might just give you a nice smile, but you can say goodbye to your € 7.70.

TIPPING

Tips are not necessary, but some tip is expected. Locals tend to round up to whole Euros. For example if a total is € 9.20, locals would just say "ten, thank you". If you're not sure, a 10% tip should be generous.

PICKING RESTAURANTS

A great way to pick your restaurant is to look for one that has some Slovak-speaking people in it. Some restaurants are just ripping-off tourists and don't really care if they will never return.

Never enter a restaurant if it's empty. It might be a sign that it's not popular or that the food won't be fresh.

SERVICE CHARGE

Some restaurants and coffee houses are so sure that their service is pristine that they include a service charge; which is basically a tip.

It's on the menu somewhere at the end and is written in small print. If you see this, there's a good chance that the whole restaurant is a rip-off, so leave. If it's too late, don't tip since you already did.

SMOKING

Since 2009, every restaurant in Slovakia has to either be non-smoking or must have a smoking room. By law, the smoking room has to be well-separated and since this is strictly monitored, it often really is separated.

Restaurants that have a smoking room tend to advertise it on their door with a sticker. When the law was established the smoking room was required to be smaller and thus, most simply banned smoking instead of building a designated smoking room.

Smoking is unregulated at coffee houses and there are only few that are non-smoking.

DRESS CODE

Except for the most exclusive places, no dress code is enforced in restaurants. If you have shoes and shirt you are welcome.

Similarly, there is no set dress code rule when attending church. Although you might be frowned upon if your dress is too short or you are showing too much.

SOUPS

KAPUSTNICA

The most popular soup is a sauerkraut soup (Slovak: Kapustnica) simply because sauerkraut was able to be stored in large quantities and also because it provided the necessary vitamin C to prevent scurvy; a disease resulting from deficiency of this vitamin.

The soup is sour and might have sausage, potatoes and sour cream in it. It is served with a few slices of Slovak bread.

BEAN SOUP

Another popular Slovak soups is bean soup. Several variations exist and most of them are thickened with a mix of sour cream and flour. Potatoes, bacon or smoked-meat are often added.

Bean soup is very tasty. If you are not adventurous with food, this soup is what you should order.

TRIPE SOUP

Slovak: Držková. This is very popular amongst older rural generations. The soup made of tripe, the wall of animal stomachs. Order it if you are more brave than you are hungry.

GOULASH SOUP

Goulash is a Hungarian meal, but it is also very popular in Slovakia; especially in the southern part. It is a stew-like soup of meat and vegetables seasoned with paprika and other spices.

It is often made using several types of meat cut to chunks and cooked with potatoes, onion, garlic, carrots peppers, celery. Hot chili peppers might be added. It is served with slices of bread.

GARLIC SOUP

Slovak garlic soup is a very flavorful soup. It is really just a garlic broth seasoned with salt, cumin and various spices. It might be served in a bread loaf.

This soup is great if you have a cold, since it's very hot and the garlic will open your airways. Just don't eat it before you have a meeting as the garlic smell is very strong.

MAIN DISHES

BRYNDZOVÉ HALUŠKY

The most "Slovak" of all dishes. The "halušky" are boiled gnocchi-like dumplings made from potato dough. It is covered with Bryndza, a soft sheep cheese. Then, bits of cooked bacon along with the bacon fat are often placed on top.

This dish is popular amongst the Slovak population. We recommend you try it out if you get a chance. Bryndzové halušky are on the menu of the majority of Bratislava's restaurants. Some even offer several variations; for example, with sausage or sauerkraut.

Traditionally, this dish is accompanied with žinčica, a sour sheep milk. While the bryndzové halušky is definitely edible, žinčica might be a bit hardcore.

▲ Bryndzové halušky with a cup of žinčica

LOKŠE

▼ Lokše

Lokše are thin, flat salty pancakes made from potato dough and cooked without oil in a pan on the stove.

They are considered as a side-dish and are served with cooked goose or duck, but people often eat them as a snack. Most restaurants don't carry Lokše, but they may offer them seasonally in the fall; which is considered duck season. You can buy them at the Christmas market during December on the Main Square (MAP ▲ 3).

The basic type of lokša is served with goose fat, while the more expensive ones are stuffed with goose liver. Stands at the Christmas market even offer sweet variations, for example with nuts.

ŽEMĽOVKA

This meal is kind of weird, but it shows how people used everything that was left in the kitchen and didn't throw anything away.

Žemlovka is similar to bread pie. It is made by mixing old bread rolls or bread with apples and cottage cheese. The ingredients are then baked.

PARENÉ BUCHTY

You might have never eaten anything like this. These are large steam-cooked dumplings with filling inside. The filling is most often jam or poppy seeds.

Parené buchty are served after pouring sweet water, melted butter and cocoa powder on top. Adding water might seem odd, but it actually improves the taste.

HARUĽA

Haruľa is a dialect name for potato pancakes. It might seem similar to lokše, but it isn't. These are much thicker and the dough is made from raw potatoes and the pancake is fried instead of cooking it on a hot plate without oil.

Haruľa is a traditional dish that is quite easy to make. The downside is that it's often soaked in oil. So, if you are not a lumberjack in central Slovakia, just try one or two.

GRANADÍR

"Granadír" or "Granadiersky pochod" is an interesting dish consisting of boiled potatoes, cooked pasta and diced and fried onions. These ingredients are mixed and seasoned with paprika and salt. Granadír is often served with pickles.

This dish is popular and Slovak families cook it frequently.

RYŽOVÝ NÁKYP

Another traditional Slovak dish, that might seem weird. It's basically rice cooked in sweetened milk and then baked in an oven and served with canned fruit. It might look like a desert, but it is not.

Are you a hockey fan? Boston Bruins captain Zdeno Chára ate at Ryžový nákyp during the Stanley cup in 2011.

SLOVAK DESSERTS

Sweet items have a rich history in Slovakia. Traditionally, grandmas didn't do anything other than bake various sweets to make their grandchildren happy (and fat). That is why there are hundreds of recipes for cakes, pastries and sweets. The reason why the recipes have a history is because nearly all of them use jams, nuts or honey and none use chocolate. This is because the grandmas we are talking about didn't have cocoa trees, so they couldn't make any chocolate and importing ingredients wasn't an option.

ORECHOVNÍK

This dessert is shared with a couple of other nations. It is known as "nut roll". Basically, it is a dough covered with nut-filling and rolled and baked. It differs from Strudel in the type of dough.

A couple of variations exist. The most popular uses poppy seeds instead of nut filling.

TRDELNÍK

A desert originating from Záhorie, a region to the north of Bratislava. It is believed that it was brought into this region by a Transylvania cook in the end of the 18th century.

It is made from a dough wrapped around a wooden stick and placed over fire. Once it's cooked it's covered with sugar and nuts.

It is very popular both amongst locals and foreign tourists.

VETERNÍK

Nearly all patisseries in Slovakia carry this cake. It consists of a bottom and a top part made of dough filled with two types of cream. The top part is covered in caramel or sugar glaze.

It gained popularity during Communism. Nowadays, it has been slowly pushed out by other types of more marketable cakes.

LASKONKA

Another Communist cake is Laskonka. This is one of those types of food that you either hate or love. Its top and bottom are hard baked and there is cream in the middle. The dough for the top and bottom parts is made simply by mixing flour, egg whites and sugar. The cream in the middle is just egg yolk and sugar.

Basically, the whole cake is just a little flour, eggs and sugar.

BEER

Beer is popular in Slovakia. The average person drinks 84 liters of beer per year; which is half that of an average Czech drinker. The majority of Slovak people prefer local brands over imported ones. This is often due to the fact that Slovak beers are cheaper.

SLOVAK VS CZECH

While tourists tend to rate Slovak beer below world-class brands like Pilsner or Budweiser, some say that Slovak beer is underated. You should definitely try it yourself.

ALCOHOL VOLUME

The majority of Slovak beer is marked 10° or 12°. This value represents the sugar content in wort, a stage of beer before fermentation. 10° beer usually contains around 4% of alcohol by volume and 12° contains around 5% abv.

BREWERIES

Most of the Slovak breweries were bought by international interests. Breweries owned by Heineken International produce more than half of Slovak output. There is one brewery in Bratislava, Stein; which makes beer according to its 1873 recipe.

▲ Copper tanks at the Bratislavský Meštiansky pivovar (MAP ▲K3)

TANK BEER

Recently, pubs started offering so-called "beer from a tank". It is an alternative distribution system where the beer is stored in huge copper tanks instead of smaller kegs. This way, beer can be unpasteurized; which makes it better tasting. How does this work? The beer is stored in large, sterile polypropylene bags placed in a copper tank. Air pressure inside the copper tank pushes the beer up to a happy customer.

▼ You can try an unusual bath at the Beer Baths BBB Prešpork (MAP ▲F5)

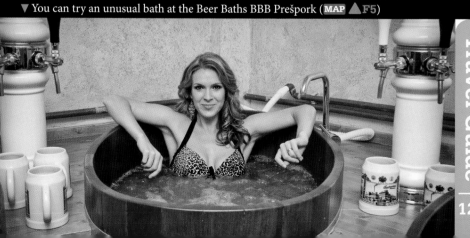

WINE

Slovak wines are not internationally known, but they are vastly popular domestically. There are six wine-producing areas, all of which are located along the south border of Slovakia. The Malokarpatská wine region is the closest to Bratislava.

WINE ROUTE

If you are a wine fanatic, various wine routes are offered where you go from one cellar to another to taste their wine. Bring a designated driver or buy a tour package that includes transportation.

The availability of tickets for this route is extremely limited and you might have to buy it well in advance.

📅 Nov 📞 +421 33 6433 489 🌐 mvc.sk

TOKAJ

Tokaj is the wine-producing region in eastern Slovakia that was originally part

▲ Vineyards are just 10km from the Bratislava city-center.

▼ These botrytised grapes are used to make the Tokay wine

SPARKLING WINE

We all know that the first sparkling wine was produced in the French region Champagne. What you probably didn't know is that Bratislava was the second place that it was produced.

According to legend, an injured Napoleon soldier who was recovering in Bratislava fell in love with a local nurse. He never returned to France and instead, he started producing sparkling wine. Since it was very popular amongst nobility, it was a huge success and the factory produces sparkling wine to this day.

of the Kingdom of Hungary, but due to the Treaty of Trianon, the region was split between Hungary and Slovakia. Tokaj wine, especially the aszú variant, is a luxurious and very sweet desert wine. Expect to pay around € 150 for a 0.5l bottle.

▼ Some of the Slovak wines are really worth trying

BEVERAGES

If you are into trying new local beverages, you have got to try Kofola and Vinea. Both were produced during Communism as a substitute for Western soft drinks like Coca-cola or Sprite. They both struggled after 1989 to stay on the market and since trademarking didn't exist in the past, several companies started producing these drinks with variable quality. Later, both of these brands were trademarked and are now produced by Kofola, a.s.

KOFOLA

Kofola is a cola soft-drink that was introduced in the 60's. It became insanely popular because it was similar to unreachable cola drinks of Western culture. Slovakia is one of three countries in the world where Coca-cola is not the best selling beverage.

VINEA

Vinea is a soft-drink based on grape juice. It was invented in 1973 by a Slovak biochemist in Bratislava and is very popular both in Slovakia and Czech republic.

SPIRITS

Unfortunately, alcoholism in Slovakia is a worrying problem; especially in the rural regions where unemployment may reach 25%. The regular volume of a shot glass is 0.05 l; which might be more than what you are used to. The drink you order might also be stronger, so be careful how much you drink.

There are no dedicated liquor stores and alcohol can be bought in supermarkets. The legal drinking age is 18.

BOROVIČKA

This type of fruit brandy production started in Slovakia in the late 19th century. In the early 20th century, this drink was even exported to USA. Nowadays, it's quite popular amongst the local population; especially the older generation. It's basically just pure alcohol mixed with water and spirit made from juniper berries; which provides the aroma. It contains about 40% alcohol by volume.

KARPATSKÉ BRANDY ŠPECIAL

One of the more prominent products, Karpatské Brandy Špeciál, is a brandy made from partially-fermented wine. It matures in oak barrels for at least five years.

▼ Juniper berries provide the taste and aroma of the borovička

SLIVOVICA

Slivovica is a plum brandy popular in Slovakia. It is made from plums which are mashed and left for three months to ferment. The product is then distilled twice and left in barrels to mature. The best brands use wooden barrels and the more it matures, the higher it's valued. The rough product often contains more than 60% alcohol by volume, so it's then diluted by water to bring the level down to 40%-55%.

SUGGESTED ITTINERARIES

CITY STROLL

This is the essential walk that covers most of the main sites in one fluid stroll. Depending on how long you will admire each site, this can take as little as two hours or as long as a whole day.

TIPS

Park your car at one of the paid parking garages (📄 35) in the city-center area. Don't waste your time trying to find free street parking.

This itinerary only provides you suggestions on how to view most of the sights in one fluid walk instead of walking throught the same place several times.

Read more about the sights as you walk by them. The number next to the page icon represents where in the book you can find more about that particular sight.

If you get lost or become confused about your location, use the map on the first pages.

ITINERARY

Start at St. Martin's Cathedral (📄 55). It can be easily found by its high tower toting a golden crown at the top. Walk in and explore the interior. Afterwards, you may leave for the next stop in the direction of the bridge.

Don't walk all the way to the Danube. Instead, turn left at Hviezdoslavovo námestie. It's a prolonged square with trees and fountains. Walk through it and you will see the statue of the "Girl with a Deer" (📄 82) in the middle of the square.

The square will lead you to the Opera

▲ St. Martin's cathedral as viewed from the Bratislava Castle

House (📄 67). Also, on the way of the Danube, there is the Reduta, the building which houses the National Philharmonic Orchestra (📄 95).

The area where you stand was considered to be outside of the city fortification walls until the 18th century and one of the city gates was between the Opera House and McDonald's currently is. There is a glass structure built above the original gate, so make sure to look at it.

When you are done, proceed to the city-center. At the first intersection, notice a statue of a man looking out of a manhole in the southwest corner. This is a popular statue called Čumil (📄 85).

Continue in the same direction to the Main

▲ The Opera House

Square (📄 59). It's the heart of Old Town. Notice the fountain, the Old Town Hall and the buildings at the square's perimeter.

When you are done, walk toward the Old Town Hall's tower. There is a narrow alley to the left of the tower that leads to the Primate's Palace (📄 63).

Return back to the Main Square through the same narrow alley you came from and turn right at the end of the passage. You are now on Františkánske Square. There is a fountain called **Woman with a jug** (📄 82), **Jesuit Church** (📄 78) and **Franciscan Church** (📄 71).

Continue uphill, along the street more to the left. This will lead you Michael's Gate (📄 65). If you feel like you have time, visit the Museum of Arms (📄 91) and enjoy the view from the tower.

Walk through the gate and it's then time to visit the castle. It's a 20-30 minute walk from here. There aren't stairs, but the route is slightly uphill. If you wish, you can return to the city and go see the Danube.

After you have walked through Michael's Gate and have noticed the moat, turn left and there you will find Trinity Church (📄 77).

Continue towards the castle by following the tram rails. Make sure to watch out for trams. Walk until the rails go into a tunnel and then go uphill to Zámocká Street. Follow this street all the way up to the castle's gate. Cross the gate and you have officially reached Bratislava Castle (📄 49).

Enter the castle and if the towers are open, you might try to get into one of them for a small fee.

Walk around and when you feel like it's time to return to the city don't go the way you came. Instead, go the other way through Sigismund Gate and tour the romantic alleys.

The last stop is the New Bridge (📄 69) and the Danube. If you have some time left, visit the observation deck.

After seeing the New Bridge, you can either return to the city-center or walk along the river. There are two shopping malls (📄 99) nearby; Eurovea and Aupark.

▲ The Bratislava riverfront in 1928

SIDE TRIPS

Bratislava's Old Town is nice, but small. If you feel like you have walked over every street at least five times and you still have some time left, you might decide to explore the surroundings.

1 DEVÍN CASTLE

The castle, built on a 200 m cliff, was first mentioned in written form in 864 when Louis the German attacked Prince Rastislav in the "Castle of Dowina". The castle's position was crucial because it overlooked trade routes going along the Danube River. The stone castle we see today first appeared in 1326. In the following years, it went through around 10 different owners, ranging from King Charles I of Hungary, to King Sigismund of Luxembourg and

Ruins of the Devín Castle ▼ ▲ The Maiden Tower of the Devín Castle

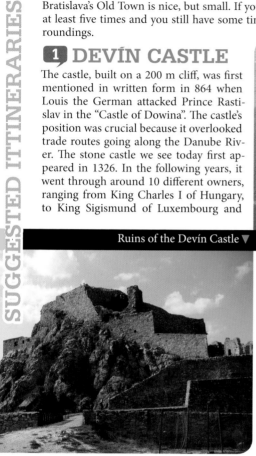

King Frederick IV.

In the 15th century, when the Ottoman armies raided Europe, a palace was added and the fortifications were made stronger. After Habsburgs defeated the Ottomans, the importance of this castle diminished.

After Napoleon besieged Bratislava in 1809, the retreating armies destroyed the castle and left it in ruins. From then on, it became an important symbol for the Slovak nation.

Visiting Devín seems like a nice day-trip. During the Communist Era, the whole area was one of the most heavily guarded in the country. It was accessible more or less only by residents. The Morava River is the narrowest here; which made it the most favored departure point for those fleeing the Regime.

A memorial arch bearing the names of those who were unsuccessful is located just a few meters from the water. Altogether, around 180,000 people successfully escaped the country, 80,000 were imprisoned for their attempts and 282 were killed while trying to escape.

The castle is open to the public; although the upper part was closed in 2008 due to safety hazards. You can get there by public transportation (📃 36).

🕐 10:00 - 17:00 📞 +421 2 65730105
€ € 3.00

2 ČERVENÝ KAMEŇ

This literally translates to "Red Stone". Červený Kameň is a beautifully-preserved stone castle; which lies 35 km to the northeast of Bratislava in Little Carpathians near the village of Častá.

The castle's history dates back to the 12th century when Constance of Hungary, a Queen consort of Ottokar I of Bohemia, had a castle built that she named Červený Kameň. The castle was later owned by several noble families.

Červený Kameň ▲

The castle was reconstructed several times and was in ownership of the Pálffy family until the end of World War II.

The preferred way to get there is by car, but a bus connection exists. Červený kameň is a venue of frequent Renaissance fairs and all kinds of family shows.

It is closed on Mondays from October-April.

(C) +421 033 690 5803 ⏰ 9:00 - 16:00
🌿 hradcervenykamen.sk 🇪 € 6.50

3 SCHLOSS HOF

This is Austria's largest rural palace complex. It is a beautiful and recently restored palace that will take you back a few centuries and show you the luxury of the Habsburg emperors.

The grounds of Schloss Hof extend over 50 hectares and include a terraced garden, orangerie and a smaller farm. The farm has over 200 animals and a petting zoo.

You can get to Schloss Hof by car or by bicycle. To get to Schloss Hof, follow the Danube Bike Trail upstream, cross the Austrian border, continue to Hainburg, cross the Danube in Hainburg and the continue

north along the local road. The trip is around 28 km one-way.

Palace tours, garden tours, pony rides and carriage rides are available.

📅 Apr - Nov ⏰ 10:00 - 18:00
🇪 € 11 (C) +43 2285 20 000
🌿 schlosshof.at

4 BOJNICE

One of the most popular travel destinations in the country is Bojnice Castle. It hosts the single most popular museum.

The castle itself dates back to the 12th century when it was built. Originally it was a wooden fort. The wooden parts were gradually replaced by stone walls. As with every castle, it had multiple owners, including Ladislaus V of Hungary, Máté Csák and even King Matthias Corvinus.

The castle underwent several reconstructions and received its present-day appearance by John Palffy who hired renowned architects and designers to make the castle similar to French castles of the Loire valley.

(C) +421 46 5430 624
🌿 bojnicecastle.sk 🇪 € 6.50

▼ Schloss hof around 1758   ▲ Bojnice Castle

IMAGES

GoGuide Bratislava - English

© 2012 Souvenir Express, s.r.o.

Author: Martin Gottweis

Proofing: Nitin Thacker

Publisher: Souvenir Express, s.r.o.

Gunduličova 4

811 03, Bratislava

www.SouvenirXPS.com

Edition: I / 2012

ISBN: 9788097101008